D0774078

LIFE ON THE EDGE

At Sea With
British Fishermen

By

QUENTIN BATES

Published by

The Hutton Press Ltd.,
130 Canada Drive, Cherry Burton,
Beverley, East Yorkshire HU17 7SB

Printed and bound by
Central Print Services the University of Hull

ISBN 1 902709 11 X

CONTENTS

Introduction

"Quentin, do you want a bit of tea?" asked the face at the shelterdeck hatch as I was heaving my bags off the quay, across the gap, and onto the boat's deck high above. After a day's travel, I was tired, stiff, and ravenously hungry.

"Yes, please. I'll just tuck the car away round the back and I'll be right with you."

A moment later the face reappeared at the hatch.

"All right, tea's on the table in the galley. But the boys say you can't have none of their sausages."

Sat squeezed into a corner seat in the tiny galley, with a row of gloves hung to dry on lengths of twine strung over the stove, the moment I saw the white enamelled plate, with three huge sausages, a generous splash of baked beans and an industrial sized portion of mash, I knew it was going to be a mistake. I did my best, not being the sort to leave much behind on a plate, but it was the sheer amount of mash that defeated me.

An hour later we were underway, steaming into a brisk wind. The boat's motion, combined with the unique fishing boat aroma that is a blend of the smells of cooking, strong baccy, drying oilskins, the engine room right underneath and the musty atmosphere, got the better of me. I made it out of the galley door and to the rail just in time, and the gulls were left squabbling in the boat's wake.

"D'you spew?" a voice from inside asked eagerly.

"'Fraid so," I had to admit.

The skipper looked out of the doorway, shook his head, smiled and said seriously, "Now, you're not going to put that in your book, are you?"

These trips all took place in 1998 and 1999, fitted in around a variety of other commitments, and most were organised on the spur of the moment. These were all trips on family owned boats, rather than on company boats. This is not something that was planned, it just worked out that way. The book is not an attempt to put together a definitive picture of the British fishing industry, I don't have the time or enough pages to play with for a fishing industry, I don't have the time or enough pages to play with for a task of that size. This is intended to be a series of snapshots, an idea of how fishermen live, work and think at the close of the 20th century. Although I have toned down the bulk of the more vigorous expletives and fruitier language throughout the book, these pages represent fishermen as they are.

There is a great deal more that I would have liked to have been able to do, and there are many areas of the fishing industry that I would have liked to have been able to cover. There are no beamers represented here, no longliners or crabbers, and there are parts of the country that I would have loved to visit, but was unable to.

The whole thing has been a battle against timetables, cars that refused to start, stubborn computers, numerous other deadlines and commitments, the weather, and like a hangover that refuses to go away, the constant threat of seasickness that is always there at the start of a trip.

My thanks to everyone who played a part in turning this book from an idea into a reality. These good people include the editors of *Fishing News*, *Fishing News International*, *World Fishing* and *Fishing Monthly*, Phil Lockley, *Fishing News'* south west correspondent, Derek Duthie of the Scottish Pelagic Fishermen's Association, Peter Moth for weeding out most of the typos, and Derek Reece at the Photo Shop in Gosport.

Above all there are the fishermen, their crews and their families who invited me on board their vessels and frequently into their homes. Taking into account the hardships that the fishing industry faces at the moment, and the general mauling that fishermen have received at the hands of the media and government, the level of unquestioning trust shown by fishermen in allowing me to poke my nose and cameras into their lives and work is little short of astounding. I can only hope that I have done them justice.

Quentin Bates
New Year's Eve 1999

Paul Joy's *Sandra* coming up to the beach after a day at sea.

1

August - *Sandra*, Hastings

Fishing From The Beach

The Stade, the fishing beach at the Sussex seaside resort of Hastings is partly hidden by rows of tarred black sheds, built tall to make best use of the limited space on the beach.

The beach is a magnet for the camera-toting trippers and foreign language students who come to Hastings in the summer months to watch the fishermen bringing their boats up the beach. But at 5 in the morning, with the stars still out, the only movement on the beach is that of fishermen going to their boats for an early start, with the quiet broken only by the hiss of waves on shingle and the grumbling of the bulldozers used to push the boats into the water.

Hastings is the home of the largest beach launched fishing fleet in Britain. Although there were plans in the nineteenth century to build a harbour for the town, these came to nothing and the fishing boats are hauled up the beach as they have been done for generations. Only the means have changed, as manpower to push the boats off was only relatively recently replaced by bulldozers, while the diesel winches at the top of the beach replaced the horse or man powered winches used in the more distant past.

A few minutes after five o'clock, with the first boats being eased into the water, I crunched across the shingle in the blackness to find Paul Joy waiting by his boat, *Sandra*, with the engine already running and ready to go. Paul peered at his watch, waiting for Ken, the crewman for the day to appear.

Paul is a slightly built man, with the bearing of a boxer and face tanned by a lifetime in the open air topped by close cropped fair hair and with bright blue eyes. He has been fishing from Hastings practically all his life, as have generations of his family in the past. The Joy family has

7

fished from the Stade certainly since the seventeenth century, and they have probably been there since long before that.

With regular crewman Ken Moss on holiday, Paul's face carried a concerned look that vanished as the relief crewman, also Ken, appeared hurrying across the shingle. A little the worse for last night's Guinness, Ken grunted a quick hello, pulled off his trainers, threw them aboard, and pulled on the pair of boots that Paul handed down to him. Between them he and Paul prepared to leave the beach, quickly greasing and pushing heavy lengths of timber, known as trows, into place behind the boat for it to run down and into the tiny waves lapping at the strip of sand further down.

Each of the forty or so fishing boats at Hastings is worked by a skipper on his own or with one or even two crewmen, but an essential part of each boat's team is a 'Boy Ashore,' who handles the bulldozer that pushes the boats afloat at dawn. At the top of the Stade is a row of sheds that house winches for bringing boats back up the beach, and this is also part of the Boy Ashore's domain.

Paul's Boy Ashore in the bulldozer gently pushed the boat into the waves, and as the stern floated, Paul put her into gear and gave some revs to bring her away from the shingle. Moments later, *Sandra* was away from the beach and steaming eastwards under the cliffs towards Rye Bay. Passing the end of the beach at Hastings, Paul slowed down to let an early morning fisherman, out in a rowing boat to drift for a few mackerel, creep back to the shore.

It was a beautiful morning. Steaming steadily towards the orange orb of the rising sun, the sea ahead was a glassy cobalt blue. With an hour's steaming ahead to pick up nets laid the day before, Paul boiled a kettle in the cubbyhole built into the back of *Sandra's* tiny wheelhouse and dished up three welcome mugs of coffee, while Ken 'Jam Buttie' sat on the gunwale and rolled himself an early morning smoke.

"It was a family business," Paul said. "The family has been fishing from Hastings back to before the sixteen hundreds. But my father thought I could do better for myself elsewhere and didn't want me to go fishing. He wouldn't allow me to go fishing, and he wouldn't sell me the boat."

Paul studied horticulture at college, qualified and for some years he had a successful business in partnership with a builder.

"He did the buildings and I did the landscaping, and we employed quite a lot of people. Then I went to pick him up for work one morning and he'd skipped off and emigrated to Australia with all the money. I'd only been working with him the day before. Then I worked with another builder, Terry Haddon, who wanted to go into fishing, and together we bought my dad's boat."

8

Soon after dawn, Paul watches from the wheelhouse for the first of the day's dahns, while Ken stands by the big nethauler.

Paul with a hand on the wheel inside Sandra's wheelhouse.

Ken brings the net through the hauler and flakes it onto the deck while Paul starts to pick the fish from the nets.

Eventually Terry's interest in fishing declined, and Paul was able to buy him out of the partnership, leaving him with his father's boat and stade.

"The first boat, RX-89, had an eight and a half horsepower engine. It was only a little open 19' boat, and it looked like a plank of wood on the water. Then Terry and I had the RX-264 between us. Terry got fed up with fishing, and I bought him out. So indirectly I'm back where I started, with the same stade as my father before me, and my father was Boy Ashore for me for a long time."

Paul expects that he may be one of the last of his family to fish from Hastings, as his sons have not chosen fishing for their careers.

"My brother has sons, and they might want to go into it, so there's that possibility. They're still quite young, but they might come into it at a later stage."

The living the Hastings fishermen make is a precarious one, with the resources they rely on varying frequently according to weather, tide and the sea temperature. A few days of cold weather at the beginning of the year can make themselves felt well into the summer, delaying the arrival of spider crabs or cuttlefish. Sometimes the fish that Hastings relies on can simply not appear, with no obvious explanation for their non appearance. In 1998 there were hardly any cuttlefish, apart from an all too brief showing, and the following year the same thing happened with the run of cod that normally shows in the autumn months. The previous year, the cod had shown, but a cod ban (later rescinded) threatened to strip the Hastings fleet of one of its most important fishing seasons.

"Last year was the best year at Hastings since the new market opened," Paul said as the *Sandra* steamed through a smooth sea towards Rye Bay and the huge square outline of Dungeness power station in the distance. "But this year has been the worst year we've had yet."

While the cod ban would have allowed fishing to continue in other areas, the Hastings boats are mostly too small to fish far from home and stick to local waters to make a living, and this would have left them to scratch for a living on out of season fish, even with the Channel full of cod waiting to be caught.

"Fish like dover sole are governed by the sea temperature. If you don't get cold winters, you don't get the fish. The fish migrate to spawn as soon as the temperature comes up, but if you don't get the cold spells, the exodus and the migration back again doesn't happen."

March, April and May are the months that the Hastings fleet catches most of its soles, but for the last couple of years, soles have not shown up in the amounts that would normally be expected.

"We've had some warm winters for the last few years, and the soles have not been showing up. But it's also got a lot to do with shingle extraction, which severely depletes resources."

In the autumn months the cod fishery normally takes over. From late October or early November the cod start to make their way down the Channel, and cod fishing can continue through to the end of January or into February.

"Last year there was a lot of cod in October, but this year there's been none at all. They spawn, and migrate back into the deep water, and we are losing them because we can't go the distance."

Another of the Hastings fleet's target species, plaice, are finished by the end of the year, and if the cod have not shown up in the autumn, there is little else until the plaice can be caught again in the spring.

Most of the Hastings boats are small and starting to show their age, and are limited strictly to fishing in waters close to home. Unlike the smaller beach fleet at Dungeness, where practically every boat is a relatively new GRP vessel capable of fishing deeper water, Hastings has been slower to renew its fishing fleet.

The newer boats at Hastings are mostly steel boats, built with a greater range and endurance than the older generation of wooden boats, which are not robust enough to withstand the rigours of scalloping, the winter fishery that has been a lifeline for many south coast boats in the last few years.

As always, the conversation turns to the politics of fishing, which are never very far away in an industry that feels itself to be as hard pressed as fishing is. Paul would dearly like to replace the aging *Sandra* with a faster GRP boat. "But the prices are colossal. That's the trend at the moment with licencing. There was a push at one time to take the under tens out of the quota system, but with the influx of rulebeaters, purpose built boats designed to plunder stocks, it couldn't be done."

"Our boats do have a limited range, ten to fifteen miles is about the limit of it, although we have been out to the Bullock Bank and the Varne. That's four hours' steam there and four hours' steam back, so that's eight hours of steaming on top of a day's work. You also have to be very careful with the weather working that far off," Paul added. Boats can be caught out by the weather and forced to make their landing on the beach in rough conditions.

Not long ago, Paul was coming in as a smaller open boat was caught badly in the surf, broadside to the waves and with its engine flooded. Paul and Ken managed to get a line across, hauled the boat clear and got the boat and its shaken crew onto the beach ashore without it losing any of its fish or gear. Almost every boat at Hastings has been damaged in the surf at one time or another, and every fisherman has stories of near misses on the beach, related in matter of fact tones.

"The boats need to be strengthened for the beach. Mine has an iron plated stem, and it's reinforced from the bow to the keel plate. We had the first bulldozer, about ten years ago. Before then it was all backs, seven or eight of us would push a boat off, then the next one, until they were all afloat. Your boat always had to lay where it was easy to move, and you couldn't push off over the sand. There were a lot of bad backs then."

With the increase in gill and trammel netting in the 1980s, and as increasing numbers of fishing boats abandoned the traditional trawl fishing, grounds such as the Bullock Bank and the Vergoyer Bank in the mid Channel became increasingly important for the quality of the soles there during the winter months.

But the combination of the distance and the vagaries of the winter weather excluded many of the smaller and slower boats from this fishery, leaving them to concentrate on inshore waters. Despite the age of the fleet at Hastings, there has been a growing amount of investment in fishing there, with a new fish market opened in 1994, and fishermen from Hastings pioneered cuttle fishing with traps.

Paul's *Sandra*, named after his wife, is one of the traditional clinker built wooden boats, built by Phillips at Rye in 1968, and was already far from new when Paul bought her. But unlike a steel boat, a wooden vessel's age is not easily determined. Paul bought the boat ten years ago, and since then practically everything has been replaced, from the old Lister diesel replaced two years ago to much of the hull, and the new nethauler fitted in last year's refit.

"We always have a refit in the summer," Paul added. "It's a lot easier if we get a couple of weeks of good weather. A lot of us would like to do it in February, as that's a bleak month with the cod gone and before the soles start. But there's no shelter and it's difficult at that time of year."

"She was an old boat when I had her, but there's no 'how long is left in a boat' with a wooden one when things can be replaced. We have the boat out every year and she's gone over with timbers and planks replaced. She's had a new deck since I've had her, a new stem, a new stern, new main timbers, and numerous planks."

Paul is one of those who has left trawling completely. *Sandra* is simply rigged only for static fishing, with only a net hauler and pot hauler. All of the masts and gantries that a trawler would carry have been long removed, leaving the deck clear for handling nets and pots. Netting has been Paul's main activity, a method of fishing that goes back many generations in Hastings.

Paul picking fish from the folds of the trammel nets.

Paul gives the word, and Ken drops the anchor over the side to shoot a fleet of nets back.

Ken sits on the gunwale to feed the net over the side, and Paul keeps an eye on the net as it drops away behind the boat.

"I've always done netting, and my father was netting many years ago. He wasn't the first to do it, but Dad was one of the first to go netting here."

"I gave up trawling really because I didn't like doing nights. In the 1980s netting came to be a lot more prominent here than trawling. Now trawling is picking up. It goes in phases. You have to be ready to change if you need to."

The fresh air and coffee did much to revive Ken from the effects of the night before, and with the sun coming up, he was ready to pull on his oilskins for the first of the day's fleets of nets.

Searching for the first of the dahns in the low slanting sunlight, Ken stood at the bow ready with a boathook, while Paul stood with one hand reaching through the wheelhouse door to the wheel, peering into the morning glare.

Paul brought the *Sandra* swiftly up to the dahn buoy, a tall bamboo cane with a float that is used to mark the end of the fleet of nets. Ken whipped the unwieldy buoy on board with practised ease, deftly stowing the pole that is almost as long as the boat itself where it would be out of the way.

The dahn line was looped quickly over the hauler, and hauled and coiled on board until the anchor, used to keep the end of the fleet of nets in position, came up to the rail. This was heaved over the rail with a grunt and dropped out of the way so that the net itself could be hauled in.

This first net was a trammel, a specialised method of fishing with a sheet of slack rigged small mesh netting and two 'outers' of much bigger mesh, which traps fish inside a bag of netting rather than catching them by the gills.

"We're using 100 mm mesh for these nets," Paul says. "It's above the minimum size, but it's something we do that's voluntary and that we believe is the right way to do it. I don't like to see too many small soles caught, even if they are legal sizes."

Ken gently hauled the net through the big Spencer Carter hauler, with the first fish flapping and glittering in the sunshine as they came round the hauler's rollers. He deftly flaked the fleet of trammels down onto the deck as Paul conned the boat along the line of the gear, until the anchor and dahn buoy at the far end had been reached and swung in over the bow.

As the *Sandra* wallowed in the slight swell, Paul left the wheelhouse to join Ken on the deck, quickly transferring the dahn rope and anchor to the starboard side and positioning the sorting bar along the deck. This length of wood is slotted into a recess at the front of the wheelhouse, and the net is passed over it as it is sorted and cleared of fish. Paul and Ken worked rapidly, freeing the fish from the bags of net that sometimes meant untwisting many feet of netting that the powerful fish had wrapped themselves in. Trapped crabs, both spiders and eaters, that had found their way into the nets were released and kept, while the smaller ones were dropped back over the side. Each fish was dropped into a box, with Paul counting a tally under his breath as they worked through the fleet, until the final net was whipped across the bar and into a heap on the starboard side of the deck ready to shoot away again.

Paul was satisfied that where his nets had been overnight had caught enough to make it worthwhile shooting back in the same place, and putting the *Sandra* into gear, brought the boat round onto the course to shoot his gear back. Ken sat himself on the rail with the anchor in his hand, and as Paul's thumbs up showed from the wheelhouse door, the anchor was dropped over the side, followed by the dahn buoy. Steaming gently, the net paid itself away over the rail, with Ken keeping a close eye on it for any of the tangles that can easily happen with lightweight gear such as this.

"Not going too fast am I?" Paul called forward from his place half in and half out of the wheelhouse.

"No, that's lovely like that," Ken replied from his seat on the gunwale, helping the pile of net leap over the gunwale to stream away into the water.

With a few minutes to steam to the next fleet of nets, Ken and I set to gut the fish, sorting soles from plaice and measuring anything that looked slightly suspect against a set of marks on a measuring board.

The last fish was dropped into the box as Paul called from the wheelhouse to announce the next fleet of nets, and within moments the dahn and anchor were on board and the process was repeating itself. This second trammel contained a similar amount of fish, but of lower quality, as the whelks had managed to find these and feasted on some of the trapped fish, sucking out the guts and leaving dead fish instead of the sprightly flapping fish that the first fleet had yielded.

As the sun rose through the morning, two more fleets of trammels and four fleets of gill nets were hauled and shot back close to where they had been before, on the edge of a hole where trawlers tow, but off the tracks that trawlers tend to work.

The cooperation between the trawlers and netters is good, and it is rare for the static gear boats to lose gear to the trawlers, although there have been rogue boats in the past from other ports that fish inside the 6 mile limit at night, sometimes towing away fleets of the inshore fishermen's nets. The loss of a fleet of gear can sometimes represent a massive loss to an inshore fisherman, and there are tales of fishermen who have been put out of business after losing the whole of their fishing gear.

Paul explained that while fishing can be good around that particular hole, if a fleet is shot into the hole itself, the steep sides are not likely to produce much of a catch. But fish coming into shallower water, and even frightened out of the hole by the activities of the trawlers, stand a chance of being caught in the overnight static nets. The state of the water also makes a definite difference, and a long spell of calm weather results in the sea being so clear that the fish can see the nets. A few spells of rough weather disturb the sea bed and cloud the water to make the nets less visible, and a few days' disturbance is also thought to stir up the sediment on the bottom and with it the smaller organisms that the fish seek out and prey on.

Although the fishing was nothing out of the ordinary, Paul was satisfied with his gear's performance where it was, and every net was shot back close to where it had been. Paul's colleague, Graham Coglan on the *St Richard*, hove into view half way through the morning. A smartly painted yellow clinker built boat, *St Richard*'s deck was loaded with the nets that Graham had decided to shift closer inshore to shoot not far from Paul's gear.

By mid morning the calm weather and gentle movement of the boat had vanished as a breeze sprang up. *St Richard* wallowed alarmingly in the swell as a shouted conversation took place between Paul and Graham, and *Sandra* rolled excitedly in the choppy sea.

"You'd forgotten how lively these little boats could be, hadn't you?" Paul called to me from where he stood in the wheelhouse with one hand on the wheel, following the line of the gear as the last fleet of gill nets was brought onto the deck. "We're real fishermen down here," he said with a wide grin. "Not like on those big boats that you're used to."

With the last of the gill nets hauled and shot, and with the fish gutted, mostly by the *Sandra*'s extra hand for the day, course was set back to the beach at Hastings, an hour away. By now full oilskins were called for on deck as Paul painstakingly went through the morning's catch, grading them by size and species into separate boxes. With the amount of water coming over the bow, there was no need to hose down the deck. In the *Sandra*'s tiny wheelhouse the kettle was put on for only the second hot drink of the day - while fishing there simply is not time to boil a kettle.

Hastings is a port without a harbour, and despite the diesel powered winches, there is still considerable labour involved in bringing a boat up the beach. On a rough day with the wind blowing from the south directly onto the beach, both leaving the beach and landing can be a hazardous undertaking. Paul was caught out two years ago when the weather worsened unexpectedly while he was at sea.

18

Paul leaving the wheelhouse to pick through the next fleet of nets.

Coming up to the beach where the bulldozer is waiting in the shallows. Paul's dog, Tyson, swims out to meet the boat.

Handing down the day's catch.

"It came on to a south-easterly force seven or eight, the worst direction for us here. We had all the gear aboard so there was a lot of weight in the boat. A big sea just smashed the side of the boat in."

On that occasion *Sandra*'s annual refit was early, and the boat was out of the water for several weeks while shipwright Eric Paine repaired and replaced the side.

Practically every one of the Hastings fishermen has found himself at one time or another stranded in the surf as things have gone badly wrong. There are hair raising tales of boats knocked sideways into the path of the breakers, and the fishermen's cafe in the market building is adorned with pictures of boats barely visible under the spray as they come ashore.

Today the surf was not more than a few gentle waves as Paul brought *Sandra* onto the shingle at low tide. Usually, the crewman jumps ashore to shackle a strop at the bow onto a wire leading through the shingle to the winch at the top of the beach, but today Paul's Boy Ashore, was waiting with the bulldozer to haul the *Sandra* the first few yards up and clear of the water, while Paul's dog Tyson was already playing in the warm shallow water.

The Boys Ashore are vital to the running of the boats, driving the bulldozers to push the boats off in the mornings, and there when the boats come in to operate the winches at the top of the beach. Each Boy Ashore gets a quarter of a crewman's share, and some handle as many as four boats.

"If a boat has seventeen shares, the crew can have four, there are twelve for the skipper and owner, and most of the skippers here are the owners as well, so there's one seventeenth left over for the Boy Ashore," Paul explained later.

Paul's Boy Ashore, Stuart Bartlett, also owns his own boat, *My Lass*, and works as Boy Ashore for himself as well as for Paul.

The bulldozer brought the boat up much faster than the winch does, and Ken and Paul toiled to keep up as it jerked *Sandra* out of the water, over the strip of sand and through the stones. As the boat made its way up the beach, Paul and Ken dragged the heavy wooden trows from behind and hauled them in front of the boat to lay them in its path, struggling to keep up with the bulldozer, which stopped a couple of times to let them catch up. By the time the boat was halfway up Ken was drenched with sweat from the exertion of keeping pace.

With the boat clear of the water, the wire to the winch was shackled in, and *Sandra* came up the shingle at a more leisurely pace to her usual resting place. Once the boat had been brought to a halt, Ken wiped the moisture from his face, grumbling that "this is a young man's game."

Once *Sandra* was firmly settled in place on the beach, Ken pulled off his oilskins and jumped down onto the shingle. Paul handed down the day's boxes of fish to waiting hands below, and a chain of men made its way up the beach, each man holding the handle of a box in each hand, so that five men carried four boxes up to the handcart outside the shed before returning for the remaining boxes.

Paul and Ken pushed the cart along the track past the rows of sheds, many of them selling freshly caught fish to the ambling trippers prowling the beach, and into the chill air of the market building. Shovel in hand, Ken heaped a mound of flake ice from the ice room onto each of the boxes of fish, which were then put away for the market the following morning.

Ashore at midday, Paul still had an hour's work on the boat, checking the engine, filling up with fuel and fetching water before stopping at the cafe for tea, a sandwich and to compare notes with the other skippers who had been coming up the beach at the same time. Most of them had finished their day's work, but Paul was still due at the offices of the Hastings Fishermen's Protection Society, of which he is the chairman.

Paul sat himself in the chair under the window, while Tyson made himself comfortable under the table.

"What time's the meeting tonight, Steve?" Paul asked.

"Seven o'clock."

"And I've got all this to do before then," Paul said, half to himself, and half to the pile of paperwork on the desk in front of him.

"Haven't even started on this," he added, picking up another sheaf of computer printouts. "Seven o'clock, you said, Steve?"

"Yes. I'll phone and remind you at half past six."

"No, don't do that. Phone me after the weather. Twenty to seven."

"Which weather do you watch then?"

"I normally watch the one on BBC."

"I'll phone you at ten to seven, then."

Paul shook his head.

"No, I'll be gone by then."

The politics of fishing takes up a vast amount of Paul's time, and he made a rapid count up of the number of committee and meetings he attends.

"I'm vice Chairman of the south east NFFO, Chairman of the Hastings Fishermen's Protection Society, joint managing director of Hastings Fish Market Ltd. I'm on the museum committee, the Stade Partnership Commission, the MSA advisory committee, and I know there's more," he said. "I'm a trustee of the Hastings Fishermen's Charity Commission, and there are council committees as well."

"You have to sit on these meetings and committee. You have to keep abreast of the trends, legislation and developments all the time, otherwise we could end up losing everything. It was mainly pressure from us that pushed the plaice sizes up," he added. "It takes a lot of time. From coming ashore, I normally come up here and this often takes the rest of the day."

Watching Paul come ashore a few days later, one of the other fishermen told me: "They don't all appreciate exactly what it is that Paul does for them here. They might have had nothing otherwise. And it's all voluntary as well."

"I've always refused to take any money for it," Paul said. "I've always been able to draw on the support of the fishing industry, and I feel that not taking a wage for this work gives me a greater credibility. It's a point of principle. Someone's got to do it."

Hastings is an example of how fishermen can work together to protect their own interests, and the Hastings fishermen have a reputation for looking after their own. The Hastings Fishermen's Protection Society (HFPS) administers the beach, allocates fishermen their Stades at committee meetings, and keeps a watchful eye on any threats to the fishermen's livelihoods.

"Twenty years ago, we had nothing on the beach. There was no electricity, no lights, and no water. If you wanted water you had to go to a public toilet for it, and at that time the Society wasn't in a position to help."

HFPS was then run in association with a fishermen's social club, without any proper organisation at all.

"What happened was that someone forgot to register the fishermen with the Town Hall, and we saw that there had to be a split with the social club, and the Hastings Fishermen's Protection Society was set up as a separate entity."

"It was a great struggle," Paul admits. "I was writing letters in the evenings, just handwritten, and you don't have a lot of credibility if letters aren't typed. Things got a lot better after Steve Peak, who is now our administrative secretary, got involved."

"The first part was to build the HFPS up into a credible organisation," Paul said. In the beginning battles with trawlers who could, and sometimes did, tow away static fishing gear brought the Hastings fishermen together, and these disputes were all resolved through the society. "All it's about is a little co-operation. We've all got to earn a living and we've all got to live together. If we have a problem here, we all act together."

Paul walking across the shingle at Hastings with Fisheries Minister Elliott Morley to attend one of many meetings that keep him fully occupied once each day's fishing is over.

Photographers, writers, film crews, scientists and politicians have all been to sea with him, and there is a steady stream of enquiries from the media for interviews and comments.

Ashore at the end of a day's fishing. Paul chats to Steve Peak of the HFPS.

Hastings fishermen have a reputation along the coast for defending their interests energetically. The loss of a couple of fleets of nets can be a severe setback to small boat fishermen whose profit margins are far from large. Fishing gear is not cheap, and the loss of several fleets of nets can represent the loss of several days fishing as well as the direct cost of the fishing gear itself.

The fishermen also enjoy an enormous level of support and popularity in the town that it is encouraging to see, and falling out with the local fishermen can result in a massive drop in popularity for any local politician. Hastings' last Tory MP found this out to her cost, especially after a scrapped fishing boat was put on the top of the beach daubed with slogans, and she promptly lost her seat. The succeeding Labour MP has been far more cautious, and has been careful to support Hastings' fishermen.

The beach itself, which belongs to the fishermen, can be used for fishing vessels, but the general public have access to it. The fishing beach is a great tourist attraction during the summer, and part of the beach is used by the local council as a car park.

Once HFPS got under way, the first move was to take out public liability insurance for the beach.

"From there we've built the Society up to stand on much stronger foundations and to be an umbrella organisation for the fishing industry here. We started the Fishermen's Co-operative here, selling gear, and we also got electricity and then water for the beach."

HFPS allocates the Stades where the boats lie, and no new ones are allocated until one is vacated. "It keeps the status quo and ensures that there's no extra pressure. That's the way it's been for the last fifty years, and that way we don't build up a fleet that's too big for the stocks. There are forty vessels here, and there are normally around thirty-five working at any one time."

"There used to be a waiting list when things were more competitive. But there's no waiting list as such now," Paul said. "Normally the Stades are handed down from father to son. A lot of the families have been here for generations."

A quick look through Steve Peak's history of fishing at Hastings shows the same names cropping up again and again, Joy, Coglan, White.

"It's not that newcomers aren't welcome, there just aren't many of them."

The local fish market was also built largely at the instigation of the HFPS. This was designed specially to fit in with the area, and the modern market building can hardly be told apart from the distinctive tall sheds built a century ago for storing and drying nets.

"There was a fish market here that was condemned," Paul explained. "There was even a possibility that the market could be shifted to Rye, so we formed a company through the local authority, consisting of fishermen and wholesalers. The fishermen had never had a stake in the market before, which the council was also steadily losing money on."

The old market, built of concrete with an asbestos roof, was condemned as soon as the new company took it over, although it had remained in use for years under the council's administration despite its condition.

"We needed to finance a new market, and as a non-profit making organisation, HFPS was the only body that was able to apply. So with the local authority we borrowed half a million, which is paid back in yearly instalments over 25 years. The market cost a million and a bit, with grants from MAFF and through the local authority. The local authority has seen the importance of seeing the fishing industry survive in Hastings."

The market has been running since 1994, and the construction of the market building included numerous other units, such as the row of fish shops on the landward side, the offices for MAFF, HFPS and several fish traders inside, a unit for a fishing gear sales firm, and Maggie's cafe. The cafe is full throughout the summer with tourists, and busy with the local fishermen through the winter as well. Maggie also opens early in the morning for the market hands, who need bacon sandwiches and mugs of tea from five in the morning. Incidentally, the local fish and chips that Maggie serves are easily among the finest to be found anywhere.

"There haven't been all that many changes over the years," Paul concluded. "There's less fish now, and there are quotas. Things have been modernized, and the emphasis used to be on trawling. There used to be a lot of punts and a few trawlers, but you have to be versatile to survive. Hastings will be the last to go. We have low overheads, with no berthing fees, *et cetera*, so we don't need a lot to survive. It doesn't need a lot of fish to make a wage for a skipper and a crew. But it is difficult to reinvest, although there are a few new boats on the beach."

"There's not many youngsters coming into it now. With unsocial hours, hard work and low pay, with a degree of education you can make a lot more elsewhere. You can't be knocked from pillar to post and have your work taken away from you by successive governments, and then expect new people to want to come into it."

Skipper Andrew Leadley taking *Carisanne* out of the harbour at Whitby.

2

August - *Carisanne*, Whitby

Searching For The North Sea Cod

I joined *Carisanne* in Whitby, a day early as it turned out. We were waiting for a technician, delayed after missing a ferry across the North Sea, to come from Denmark to repair the boat's fishroom chiller system. Whitby was packed with the annual influx of summer visitors attending the annual folk week, some dressed in the far from traditional black capes and fangs to celebrate the town's Dracula connection. A constant flow of tourists meandered along the town's dock past its fish n' chip shops, fruit machine arcades and pubs, to stare down at the fishing boats twenty feet below.

Carisanne's crew, Mike the mate, Gibson, Colin and Adam, were spending a few hours working on the boat's trawls in the sunshine, each with an eye cocked towards the trippers on the dock.

"Sometimes there's women walking along there with no knickers on," one of the crew told me with a huge grin. "But I've only had the privilege of seeing that once."

With the new compressor fitted, *Carisanne* steamed smoothly out of Whitby harbour into a gentle swell. Mike made some last minute adjustments to the gear, stringing new dollies onto new codends and splicing a couple of new strops, while the others made the boat shipshape, coiling down the mooring ropes and closing hatches. Gibb in the galley was stacking food into cupboards, and the frozen food had already been taken forward to the deep freeze in the bow. The speed with which a fishing boat can come to life is always a surprise, as the crew quickly had everything ready to start fishing.

Carisanne is one of the biggest boats to fish from Whitby. Built in Sweden a dozen years ago as the *Kätty*, she found her way to Iceland as a seine netter, *Jón Klemenz*, and then to Fraserburgh where she worked as a trawler, before being bought by Andrew Leadley in Whitby.

This is a middle water trawler, built to spend days at a time at sea, with the crew of five cleaning and storing the catch, iced in boxes, in the chilled fishroom.

This trip was intended to be a short one on grounds off the Yorkshire coast, practically within sight of land, and certainly within sight of coasters making their way to and from the Tyne or the Tees and numerous small boats carrying angling parties.

"You often see them going out with parties of miners from Barnsley, crates of beer on board, and when they come back they're all laid in the bottom of the boat," Andrew commented as we steamed out.

A few hours out from Whitby, *Carisanne*'s crew pulled on their oilskins in the narrow passage on the port side. Boots, rubber trousers and waterproof tops are stored in this passageway, and the galley has a handwritten notice which reads 'no oilskins beyond this point'. Gloves are kept on the hot pipes that run along the passage, but this never dries them out, it just turns them from cold, wet gloves into warm, damp gloves.

Carisanne sails with a crew of four or five, in addition to skipper and owner Andrew Leadley. Mate Mike Stephenson at forty is the oldest man on board, and like the rest of the crew has been a fisherman all his life, and has never wanted to do anything else. Apart from a spell as skipper of a boat for another owner in Whitby, most of his career has been spent with Andrew's family

"Mike's been with me since I had my first boat," Andrew said. "He's been here ever since, apart from a spell away when my boat was being converted."

"I started with Andrew's granddad," Mike told me later. "Then I worked for Jim, Andrew's dad, and then for his uncle Peter, and I've been with Andrew since he first got the *St Leger*."

"I've never wanted to do anything else. Some of my mates went to Hull as trainees, but I went to work with Andrew's granddad and I've been with them ever since." He added that after leaving school, there was a blockade on fishing for a while, and he spent several months in a building job. "I hated it, and left it as soon as I could," he said.

Mike's cabin has a stack of navigation and stability books on the tiny table by the door, and this is where he spends as much time as he can, snatching an hour between hauls when possible, to study for the skipper's ticket that he needs to be able to take the *Carisanne*. When Andrew takes a trip off, his father Jim and Mike take the boat between them.

"I do the book work here when I can, and sometimes I can use the galley table for the chartwork," Mike says. "The trouble is that you get halfway through something and then it's time to haul, or somebody comes along and says 'what you doing?' and your concentration's gone."

Studying is a battle for someone in Mike's position, and the only way to sit for a ticket is to study through a correspondence course. Unfortunately, Mike's tutor is also frequently at sea, and their trips ashore do not always coincide.

The rest of the crew are ponytailed Adam Chadwick, the youngest in the crew at twenty-six, Gibson 'you can tell he's the cook' Halley, and taciturn Colin Storr. On this trip, the remaining deckhands, Simon Dunne and Andrew Wilson, were both ashore.

Ready to shoot away for the first time as the sun was beginning to drop towards the horizon, Adam, Colin and Mike took their positions at the stern, while Gibb took his place at the controls for the net drums and the powerblock just aft of the wheelhouse door.

The cod end was heaved over the side and dropped away astern, and the belly of the trawl lazily snaked into the water after it. With the bellies streamed astern, Gibb stood at the hydraulics, watching and listening for shouts and signals from the stern, turned the drum to spool one of the two hard ground trawls off the drum. *Carisanne*'s aft deck is cramped, to say the least, with four net drums taking up most of the space, leaving only a few yards of deck for working on the gear. Two hard ground trawls and two soft ground trawls are carried on four drums, and the clump used for twin rig trawling is parked on the deck as well, and has to be stepped over every time anyone goes aft to the trawl deck.

The rubber bobbins of the rockhopper footrope bounced and struggled over the aft roller and into the water, with help from Adam, Colin and Mike. After the footrope, the double sweeps began to pay off the drum, with the crew risking their fingers to keep the chains and wires separate. On the last haul of the previous trip, the sweeplines had been would on unevenly, and in shooting them away again they crackled and sparked as the wires snapped their way across the mounds of heaped wire on the drum.

"Must have been bloody blind whoever put all this on last time," complained Adam and Colin, struggling to keep the wires squared away.

The chains of the sweeps were worn away in places, the links pared away thin and sharp by constant contact with the seabed. "Everything's like this," one of the crew said. "Everything's just used until it's worn right out, and we're parting wires and chains all the time. That's what it's like working for a skipper owner, nothing gets replaced until the last moment."

Shooting one of the trawls off the starboard net drum, with the crew struggling to keep the sweeplines apart.

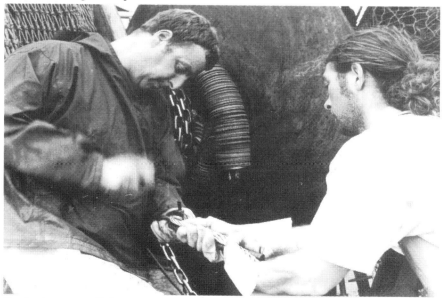

Replacing one of the sweeps, parted in the first tow of the trip. Colin Storr hammers home the pin in a shackle as Adam Chadwick holds it steady.

Deckhand Adam Chadwick tying the codend.

Mike the mate doing some running repairs to the gear between hauls. Damage is frequent, and can vary from a few meshes to a trawl in tatters.

Colin and Gibb at the gutting table

When the trawl was fully paid away and the flatlinks appeared off the drum, the backstrops were hustled round from the doors and their G links clipped in. Paying off the drum allowed the weight of the trawl to be taken onto the trawl doors, which now bucked as if they had a life of their own, still chained up at the gallows.

By this time, Gibb had gone forward to the winch under the shelterdeck, leaving Andrew on the hydraulics behind the wheelhouse, holding an intercom to relay instructions forward. He barked into the intercom, and the warps took the strain on the trawl doors, allowing the crew on the deck to unchain them ready for shooting away. As *Carisanne* gathered way, Andrew spoke a word into the intercom, and the doors dropped gently into the boat's wake.

The warps are marked at intervals, allowing the skipper to see the length of wire out. Once the right length was reached, Andrew barked again into the intercom and the winch came to a gentle halt. Adam and Mike took chain loops and slung them over the warps, winding them around the wires half a dozen times, then hooked a pair of thick chains into the loops. Another bark into the intercom to the winchman forward under the shelterdeck, and the warps were slackened off to leave the chains to take the strain of the trawl.

Andrew explained that he prefers to use a single towing point, as this is more convenient for taking a turn, with less chance of the inside trawl door lying flat on the seabed.

Once the trawl had been shot away, the boat appeared to settle into an immediate easy rhythm. The crew quickly cleared away any rubbish on the deck left over from repairs to the gear, and settled themselves in the galley with mugs of tea and the television burbling quietly in the corner. This was one of the first trips of the year on fishing grounds within television range, and decent reception was something of a novelty.

The television is a constant presence on board, with the picture flickering all day and night in a corner of the galley, only with the volume is turned up very high can it be heard properly over the relentless roar of the main engine directly below. The crew happily watch almost anything. From the moment they appear from their bunks, all eyes are drawn to the screen. Everything is welcome, children's programmes, Open University, breakfast TV and terrible game shows. Soaps are a favourite, as is practically any kind of sport, but the appearance of the Tellytubbies normally results in channels being switched fairly quickly.

"It's the same when we're working over the other side of the North Sea and they're watching something in Dutch or German," Andrew said.

"You ask 'what's this', 'don't know', 'how long's it been on?', 'about two hours', 'any good?', 'no, it's rubbish.'"

"Fucking hell!" Someone swore as the winch engine was heard starting up, and the whole crew abandoned mugs of tea and sandwiches to struggle into oilskins again, less than half a hour after shooting away.

"We've come fast," Andrew said as I appeared in the wheelhouse. "We'll have it up and check the trawl. If it's all right we'll just shoot straight back again."

The warps were quickly unchained and the winch ran the warps aboard until the doors appeared at the towing blocks. The pennants were snapped off the doors and clipped into the leader chains on the empty drum, and the sweeps began to wind on.

"Parted a sweep!" Mike called as the splits appeared. Just the eye of one of the double sweepline wires dangled from the end of the single sweepline, leaving a wing of the trawl trailing back inside the net. A replacement was hurriedly fetched from below, and shackled into place, then the rest of the trawl was struggled aboard to retrieve the end of the wing.

The trawl was shot back, and this time the tow was completed without any more damage to the gear, although the first tow of the trip was a disappointing one. The trawl's footrope was brought onto the drum, far enough to reach the lazy deckie, a rope that leads down to the belly of the trawl. This was slung around the powerblock, and the belly hauled in. Adam tied it off quickly, and he and Colin stood at the stern under a stream of water dripping from the net as it was dropped back. With the lazy deckie retrieved, the belly was thrown over the powerblock again and the net hauled in to bring the codend to the surface. Andrew manoeuvred the boat the keep the floating codend of the trawl clear of the side, while Mike swung a grappling hook to fish the line leading to the becket around the cod end clear of the water. This line was hooked into a gilson and the bag of the trawl hauled clear of the water and into a bay forward on the starboard side. The codend swung into its frame of retaining bars as the water streamed from it and Adam groped between the edge of the hatch and the bulging bag of fish to find the codline. With a grunt and a series of quick pulls, he released it to let the glittering fish fall into the steel pound.

Cod, haddock, whiting, plaice and lemon sole lay flapping their lives out until the crew had shot the trawl again and were ready to deal with them. Andrew watched impassively from the wheelhouse window as Adam and Mike strained to pull the codend onto the deck and Adam tied the codline again with movements so quick that the eye could barely follow them.

36

Breakfast time, and still in TV range.

Andrew at the wheelhouse window.

"How much was that, then?"

"Not a lot."

The codend dropped away again and snaked into the distance as Andrew put *Carisanne* into gear and the crew prepared to shoot away again. With the trawl back in the water, Gibb made his way below to the winch, waiting for Andrew's barked commands over the intercom speaker above his head.

He carefully hauled in and slacked out short lengths of warp as the doors were brought up to the gallows and unchained, finally letting go to slack off the warps as the winch itself juddered and shook.

"This bloody thing's going to come loose one day," he shouted over the rattling of the winch.

Carisanne's shelterdeck is a luxury that gives the crew protection from the weather while they are busy sorting and gutting the catch. Unlike older boats, where all of this work is done in the open, the crew can strip down to tee shirts while they work. In bad weather a shelterdeck is a god-send, both in terms of comfort and safety.

Once the trawl was back on the bottom, the crew came back inside, rolled fags and made their way to the gutting table. Mike opened a small hatch in the pound to let a stream of flapping, gasping, shining fish onto the bare stainless steel table. Working with rapid movements, waste fish, those too small to keep, or simply those not worth keeping, were consigned to baskets to be dropped back over the side through the waste hatch, while the majestic big green cod, the silver haddock with the devil's thumbprint on their sides, golden brown lemons and the rusty patched plaice were shoved along the table to the razor sharp, short bladed gutting knives wielded by Gibb and Colin.

Occasionally there's a turbot, deep green above, with hard knobbly skin and a pearly white belly, and as big as a suburban coffee table. These are carefully cut at the tail to allow them to bleed, before being gutted and painstakingly washed by hand. Turbot are too valuable to be handled roughly, with each box fetching as much as £500.

Gibb and Colin worked with practised speed, slitting round fish from throat to belly in a single movement, and slipping the guts onto the table, holding a constant ribald conversation all the time. Each fish is then dropped into the right basket, or tossed straight into the washer. Even before the fish get as far as the washer, another fish is already half gutted. Standing between Colin and Gibb and out of practice, I only managed to gut and clean one fish for every two that they each dispatched with knives sharp enough to shave with. Flatfish are sliced across behind the head, and the gut extracted in a single movement. Badly out of practice, in ten

38

minutes my thumb was aching with the effort of keeping lemons, sole and plaice still in one hand long enough to be gutted as they wriggle and twist away from the knife.

As we began work on the fish, a disappointing haul, according to the others, a speaker behind us burst into life, and the crew gutted to the sound of Four Non Blondes crashing their way through Bigger, Better, Faster, More.

Gutting is a shock to the uninitiated. Watching fish gasp out their short lives on a gutting table, before being ruthlessly slaughtered is not a sight for the squeamish. Piles of fish guts collect on the table, and the steel table runs red with the blood of cod and haddock before it is all sluiced away. For me, not being a newcomer to fishing, I was more disturbed by the amount of fish that is discarded. Piles of small fish are shovelled over the side to the waiting gulls, who follow trawlers to pick up the dead fish and guts left in their wake.

The birds are always there following fishing boats, and a boat that has just hauled can be easily identified by the flocks of squawking gulls around it. While they are normally graceful creatures that soar and swoop behind the boats, anything edible discarded by the boats turns the gulls into squabbling, screeching beasts, vicious enough to steal food from each others' mouths.

Each haul followed the same pattern. As soon as the trawl has been shot back, the crew made their way forward to gut the fish. Adam, who always stopped to roll a smoke on his way aft, put on a CD from the collection in the galley to blast out while the fish are dealt with, before making his way to the fishroom. He is also always the last to make his way back to the galley, emerging from the fishroom some time after the last fish has been gutted and the washed fish have been sent below.

The fishroom is Adam's domain, and the quality of the trip's fish depends very much on the skill and care of the man who ices and boxes the catch.

The fishroom is dim, lit by a couple of weak lights, and chill enough to take your breath away. At the start of the trip, boxes were stacked forward, and as the trip progressed, the number of full ones stacked against the aft bulkhead grew satisfyingly.

Adam treats each fish with plenty of tender loving care, lining them up in boxes so that they drain properly and so that they get the maximum benefit of the crushed ice that is shovelled liberally into the bottom of each box and onto the top as each box is filled.

The icemaker on the deck above needs to be watched regularly to ensure that the chute to the fishroom is not blocked. The ice maker was fitted recently so that the boat would not have to rely on ice taken at the start of each trip from an ice plant ashore. It produces a constant stream of crushed flake ice, which collects in the fishroom ice pound. Without the ice, fish would not keep for more than a few hours in hot weather.

With the fish put to bed, the crew make their way back to the galley for the first of many mugs of tea. A mug is taken up to Andrew in the wheelhouse, and the galley television is switched back on.

"Good one tonight," Adam says. "Coronation Street first, then switch over to Eastenders and see what those brothers are planning."

Fishing continues around the clock, and the crew snatch sleep between hauls, retiring to the cabins in the *Carisanne*'s stern. Every four or five hours, everyone is up and the gear brought aboard. Those four-in-the-morning hauls and struggling into cold oilskins still damp from the last haul were things that I thought I had left behind me, at least for the time being...

But everything, sleep patterns, mealtimes and anything else on board revolves around hauling and shooting, and this trip was a relaxed one with plenty of time to catch a couple of hours sleep between hauls.

"It wasn't like this last year," Adam said ruefully. "It was always full, and you used to pray for a bad haul so you'd get a few hours sleep." But a fisherman's earnings are directly linked to the catch, and they would all clearly have preferred to have been sleeping less and working more.

The wheelhouse is the skipper's kingdom. Andrew rarely left it throughout the trip, except to snatch a few hours' sleep while leaving one of the others to take half of a tow. Meals and mugs of tea are carried up to the wheelhouse for Andrew to consume in the chair facing the array of electronic wizardry.

Carisanne's wheelhouse, like most fishing vessels, carries enough electronic equipment to put most merchant ships to shame. Positioning is vitally important, and clipping a wreck can mean the difference between a sizable bag of fish and several hours' work mending a paralysed trawl. Directly in front of Andrew's chair is the colour echo sounder, flanked by a plotter which is linked to one of the boat's GPS receivers. This makes it possible for Andrew to plot his position, and the positions of seabed features such as wrecks and other fasteners.

One night in the wheelhouse Adam was taking the watch while Andrew snatched a few hours' sleep. The track the boat was following could be seen on the plotter, some way from the tow that Adam was trying to follow. Peering out through the back window of the wheelhouse, the towing chains were leading well away to port as the boat struggled to come round.

Adam throws the lazy deckie over the powerblock to bring the codend up.

Fishing around the clock. Colin shackling the backstrops into the flatlinks on the sweeplines in the middle of the night.

More damage this time as Andrew and Mike mend their way down each side of a gash in one of the wings.

Adam boxing cod in *Carisanne*'s fishroom.

"Come on you fucker..." Adam muttered under his breath. "She's taking a while to get round. Turning into the tide doesn't help either," he added as the boat swung against the force of the current to follow the nest of tracks of previous tows on the plotter screen.

It had already been a difficult year for the crew of the *Carisanne*, and their fishing grounds had taken them all over the North Sea. "Last year was very good," Andrew said at the start of the trip. "We rely heavily on cod for our fishing, and we hardly had to go more than twenty miles off for most of the year, but this year the inshore grounds have been barren. It's gone from boom to bust in a year. This year it's been fair to a pain, very poor fishing on the inshore grounds, but the better price has helped. Last year there was quite a boom, though," Andrew said. "The inshore boats are surviving on price alone, and if it were to drop and further..." He left the sentence unfinished.

Fishing along undersea pipelines is something that tends to produce good catches, and these are carefully marked on charts. A sidescan sonar on board is used to help make sure that the trawl stays in place. "We tow up to the pipeline so that one door jumps over, then you bring her hard around to keep the other one from going across," Andrew explained. With the doors either side of the pipe, and the trawl straddling it, the sonar with its transceiver towed behind one of the doors clearly shows both doors with the pipeline between them.

"We have even resorted to prawning this year. The only limit to what you can catch is how fast you can clear them off the deck, and the crew hate it. The crew are on deck from when you start to when you've had enough. We did it a lot the year before last, but last year with the good cod fishing, we didn't bother. You enjoy prawning, don't you Chaddie?" Andrew asked Adam, who had just appeared in the wheelhouse.

"Lovely job. Oh yes," Adam replied, clearly not keen to see another prawn ever again.

Later he told me that prawning isn't popular with crews and the hours on deck are longer than with any other kind of fishing.

"Good earnings? No, it's shit. We were filling that hopper right to the top every time. I thought Simon was going to chuck himself overboard last time we went prawning. He must have nightmares about prawns."

Andrew pointed to a small winch on the foredeck. "We used to use that winch for the codend, with just a handle on the deck instead of going through all this rigmarole with the main winch to get the codend up. But we broke that winch last time we went prawning. She was laid over a bit, and I don't know which was groaning most, the winch or the crew."

He added that with fishing of that intensity, it is important to stop for a few hours each day to allow the crew some sleep. Trips also tend to be shorter, and two days prawning is normally enough.

"I prefer to go twin rig fishing for whitefish with some bycatch of prawns, as opposed to out and out prawning," Andrew says. "It's a lot better if there's some fish to gut as well."

Carisanne uses a scraper trawl with 100 mm mesh in the codend for prawn fishing, but for any other fishing, 110 mm mesh is used, larger than the legally required minimum size. "Our trawls are the standard Whitby design, and 100 mill is the mesh size for what we are fishing," Andrew says. "But there were a lot of small codlings on the grounds last year, and I just can't see the point in killing them."

"These are traditional Whitby cod grounds, supposedly, where we are now, but they are just not in at the moment. There was a huge amount of fish caught up to Christmas, then it just turned off. It was an exceptional year for cod," he said, and admitted that the year's grossing for the boat was a respectable figure, but declined to give a precise amount. "We were averaging £10,000 a week. The expenses are paid and the rest is split half and half with the crew."

"Last year was really good," Adam told me while we were waiting for the doors to come up. "Sometimes you'd be praying for a slack haul so you could get some sleep."

1999 was very different, with local grounds largely barren, and Andrew was forced take *Carisanne* further afield. "At one time fifty miles from Whitby was as far as you'd go, but we have become more nomadic, and now we go wherever we have to. There is a growing trend for things to get tighter, but there is still a living to be made. It's not so much that the job is harder, but it is different."

This trip was a local one, keeping between ten and twenty miles form the Yorkshire coast all the time, sticking to mostly rocky ground. The twin rig gear and the larger fine ground trawls with their longer sweeplines were not used at all, and several times there was damage to the two hard ground trawls.

"Further in the ground gets even harder," Andrew said. "We've gone from the east edge of the fine ground to the west edge of Baymans this trip. If we go north of the Tees, you get into prawning grounds, and go ten or fifteen miles south and you're into ground where the whelkers work."

Carisanne has taken Andrew and his crew over much of the North Sea, across to the German Bight and into the Norwegian sector, an area that he avoids if possible, largely due to the difficulties of dealing with the Norwegians, who apply onerous rules and controls on boats fishing in their waters. "If we can complete a trip without going up there, we will," Andrew said. He has also taken *Carisanne* over to Holland to fish for red mullet in the spring off the German and Dutch coast, and landing catches in IJmuiden.

"We did very well there during the food scare in Belgium. Prices were sky high at one point, and I even saw a Dutch beam trawler skipper with a smile on his face when he got his sales note for one trip."

For the rest of the year, *Carisanne* lands fish to Scarborough market. Whitby is not a designated port, one of the harbours that are part of a scheme introduced by the authorities to crack down on landings of illegal 'black' fish.

"If we land at Whitby, we have to book in in advance, and we have to do the same at Scarborough, unless we land between eleven at night and seven in the morning," Andrew says with a shake of the head. "If you were going to be doing something illegal, that's when I'd have thought you'd want to do it. These designated ports don't appear to have made a vast amount of difference."

"I'm also in the ridiculous position of seeing the fishery officer on the quay there. So I have to take my log sheets along the quay, closely followed by the fishery officer, so that I can post the log sheets into the post box. Then the fishery officer opens the box and takes the sheets out. I'm not allowed to just hand him the log sheets," he says with another shake of the head. "It's all part of the ridiculous rules and regulations that they have to go through the motions of enforcing."

He added that most of the fishing boats along the Yorkshire coast have been investigated for tax evasion, and he himself was under investigation for two years. "I think they expected to find untold millions of pounds worth of black fish somewhere, but all they managed to come up with was a little bit of stocker money. It's something that they decided to do, and they have been through each port in turn." He added that his accountant's fees will probably be greater than the fine for the very minor irregularities that were found.

The sheer amounts of paperwork and regulation have escalated alarmingly over the past decade. Twenty years ago the level of regulation amounted to little more than mesh sizes and minimum landing sizes, but this has all changed, and the weight of bureaucracy represents a growing burden.

"It is getting heavier all the time," Andrew says. "They started bringing in all these rules at about the time that I got my first boat, so it's maybe easier for me that for someone who had already been able to do what they wanted for twenty years."

"The biggest pain in the arse is the MCA (Marine and Coastguard Agency). This boat was flagged in from Iceland in 1995 by surveyors in Scotland, and when it went through its last DTI, I was told that it shouldn't have been accepted. One surveyor's application of the rules doesn't always seem to be the same as another's. The DTI cost £2500 in MCA fees alone, which included a grey area called 'office fees'. Quite what that is I'm not sure." "There seems to be some kind of power struggle between the older and the younger surveyors, and the fishermen are caught in the middle."

As the trip progressed several other boats from Whitby and Scarborough appeared on the fishing grounds, and at night a string of lights along the coast could be seen clearly twinkling in the distance.

On the second day of the trip, with the crew working on mending a trawl that had been shredded on hard ground, one of them pointed to a shape heading towards us that was rather different to the usual coasters and fishing boats all around.

"Is that the fishery boat, Mike?"

"Looks like it. I'd better go and tell him."

Mike made his way up to the wheelhouse, and Andrew put his head through the door to peer at the ship that had clearly altered course towards us.

I asked if it would be all right to go on taking pictures and notes if we were boarded.

"Oh yes, take pictures of what you want. As long as you don't take one of me being taken away in handcuffs," he said with a thin smile. "They always seem to come straight to us and I don't really know why. I suppose it might be because of the Fraserburgh registration."

This time the fishery protection vessel steamed past close enough for the evening sun to be able to pick out every detail of its hull and equipment. Mike peered at it as it cruised past, looking intently to see any activity on board that could indicate a boarding party on the way.

"Looks all right. They haven't got a boat over," Mike said happily, and the ship pulled past us and away. "Going into the Tyne for a long Bank Holiday weekend, I expect," Andrew said, as the other ship had clearly set its course for Shields.

Mike, Colin and Adam went back to mending the trawl on the deck, braiding new net onto the holes torn in the trawl's wings, while Gibb in the galley was getting the evening meal ready.

Not long past thirty, Andrew has been at sea all of his working life, leaving school at fifteen to join the *Kristand Jo*, father's boat. Unlike the bulky men who make up the rest of the crew he is slightly built, not a man who would be picked out in the street as a deep sea fisherman. He has a quiet manner and a voice so low that it's sometimes an effort to hear what he says. All the same, there is something about his bearing that shows unmistakably that he is used to being in charge.

Only once during the trip did any anger show, when one of the crew had taken the latter half of a tow, and the gear came up with a wing badly torn and the codend chafed out by a boulder picked up in the trawl.

"Fucking hell! Mike, the fucking codend's out!" The sheer frustration in his voice was unmistakable and the rest of the crew went about with a slightly greater speed than usual to get the gear aboard.

Fish were dropping out of the codend as it emerged form the water, and a couple of big cod swam slowly away in triumph. Only a basket of fish was saved from the haul, and the crew quickly switched trawls while Andrew swore to himself.

Andrew explained that his family had already been in fishing for many years, and older brother Steve was expected to become the skipper of the family until he lost a leg in an accident. "That was when I was fifteen, and it seemed to be the expected thing after that that I would take the family boat."

"Me and school didn't get on," he went on to say. Despite being due to take eleven O levels and being encouraged to go on to further education, he rebelled and went early, burning his boats behind him and leaving with no qualifications. "As soon as there was a job on my father's boat, I took it. My first week's wages paid the fine for not going to school." By the time he was nineteen, he was taking the boat on trips and had his own 60' boat at twenty-two.

Asked if he would expect his own sons to become fishermen, he replied that he would be happy to take them on board when the time comes. "But only if they show an interest in running their own boat. There isn't a lot of point in doing it otherwise. I always aimed to be up here as soon as possible," he says, looking around the boat's wheelhouse. "It's having the freedom to make your own decisions that is important."

"My old boat was very basic, to say the least," he added. "There was no shower, no toilet, no real galley. She was quite old, built twenty years

47

Gibb in the fishroom, dragging the full boxes of fish under the hatch to be landed.

Colin steadies the boxes as they are swung onto the quay.

Fish buyers on Scarborough market as *Carisanne*'s fish is landed. Despite the uninterested expressions, everything was sold at a good price.

before, one of seven or eight boats for the same owners and built for inshore fishing, and wasn't exactly a state of the art fishing boat."

This was the *St Leger*, which Andrew later had stripped to the deck, covered and fitted with a shelterdeck, and renamed *Samantha L.*

This boat was bought for £180,000. "At that time you bought a boat and the licence came with it, and wasn't much more than a piece of paper that didn't mean a vast amount."

A few years later Andrew sold the boat alone to Mallaig for a substantial figure, and the licence for more than double that amount to four boats in the PO which split the fish allocation between them. The boat is now back in Whitby, as the *Good Intent*. The amount of money that a licence costs in today's fishing industry is phenomenal compared to a few years ago. "It's impossible for anyone to make a start in this industry now as a newcomer," Andrew commented.

Carisanne was bought to replace the *Samantha L.* The boat was fishing from Fraserburgh for an owner who had brought it to the UK from Iceland, and who wanted to move on. "She was going to be sold back to Iceland, but she had already been decommissioned there and the buyer found that he couldn't import the boat back to Iceland again, so the deal fell through. I'd just sold my old boat and happened to be in Fraserburgh at the time, so I was in the right place at the right time," Andrew explained.

"I suppose I could sell up and live comfortably," he admitted. "But what would I do? I do enjoy fishing and I'd only have to find some other masochist thing to do."

Carisanne was bought in 1996, and is now one of the largest fishing boats working from Whitby. "She has a lot more range and capacity than the old boat. She's a lot more comfortable for spending long periods away from home. We can go where we want and do what we have to, or we would if it wasn't for all the rules and regulations."

A stern trawler like the *Carisanne* is far more versatile, is capable of working in bad weather under tough conditions, and is considerably safer than a side trawler, especially when trying to get loose from a fastener.

"There's some quite hard ground inside two miles, and they used to say that you couldn't jump a stern trawler off a fastener, but all you have to do is go astern. There are only a few side trawlers left in Whitby now," Andrew said, and added that work on deck on a side trawler is far harder and more exposed for the crew. "If I asked this lot to haul in a net by hand, they'd look at me as if I was mad."

Crew can be a problem at times. *Carisanne* has its regular crew working their two trips on and one off system that allows each crew member one trip in three ashore. "We normally carry a trainee as well, but our last one did a runner and we're between trainees at the moment. You have to go through about twenty trainees to find one good one," he added.

Carisanne's crew have been together for a good while, and they have all been on the boat for a year or two, or like Mike the mate, a lot longer. "It doesn't seem to matter how much you put in their hands," Andrew said. "It's the same if it's £1500 or £500 at the end of a trip, they keep coming back."

In general, crewing a trawler is not always so easy. "When they are earning £1000 a week, you're beating them of with a stick and you have a waiting list for crew. But when the fish are scarcer, so are crew. There are a lot of fair weather fishermen in Whitby," Andrew commented, meaning fishermen who stick with a boat through good fishing but leave a boat as soon as earnings drop.

Meals come twice a day on the *Carisanne*. Gibb dishes up a breakfast soon after the morning haul, and a second big meal at the end of the day, except that on a fishing boat like this there is no 'end of the day' with fishing continuing around the clock, so a meal appears late in the afternoon, depending on when the gear is hauled.

Each meal makes its appearance on the galley table in a deep steel dish, so there is less chance of food sliding off the plate in sloppy weather, and no chance of the plate breaking if it does hit the deck.

"There's a nice plate of cholesterol for you," Mike said as Gibb handed me my first breakfast on board. Two fried eggs, sausages, bacon and two burgers jostled for position in the dish, with an extra dish of beans and tomatoes in the middle of the table for everyone to dip into. The evening meal is solid food, steak, pies, chicken, with potatoes or chips, and normally beans again. This is not health food in any way, but high energy food for people doing hard work for long hours, often in exposed and cold conditions. Every meal is accompanied by numerous rounds of bread and butter, and much of each meal becomes a makeshift sandwich, with sausages, chips or meat crammed between slices of bread. Most meals are also showered with a bewildering array of sauces from the rack of bottles at the end of the galley table. Brown sauce and vinegar are staples, but mint sauce spread onto roast chicken is just as likely.

Fish is a rarity on the galley table, and only normally eaten when meat is running short. On the last day of the trip, I persuaded Gibb to cook some fish, and that evening's meal was the finest of the trip with deep fried haddock so fresh it was practically still flapping on the plate. However, not all of the crew are keen on fish, and a plate of sausages, fried in the same oil as the fish, also disappeared quickly between slices of bread.

After almost a week at sea, and after extending the trip by a day to avoid landing on a Bank Holiday, Andrew brought *Carisanne* into Scarborough early in the morning to land the catch at the local fish market, with the boat short enough of fresh water for a shower to be out of the question.

"Fucking late again," one of the crew grumbled. "Should have been in last night. But he can't steam anywhere, always has to tow from one place to another, his Dad taught him that."

The boat was edged up to the quayside, and as soon as *Carisanne* was tied up, the fishroom hatches in the shelterdeck and the main deck were lifted off and the first boxes were swinging ashore with Mike working the winch. Colin steered the stacks of boxes through the hatch while Adam and Andrew waited on the quay. Gibb was down in the fishroom, beaded with sweat as he struggled with the heavy boxes of fish to stack them under the hatch. Each block of boxes swayed up, was spun round at the hatch opening and lifted up to be hauled ashore. As soon as the boxes hit the quay, lumpers from the market were ready with their iron box hooks to drag them inside to the waiting buyers, staring unappreciatively at the rows of white boxes and sipping plastic cups of steaming tea.

This was the end of the trip, and as soon as the fish were ashore, Mike and I made our way to the taxi to take us back to Whitby, while the rest of the crew were still getting *Carisanne* ready to sail again that afternoon.

Contrary to the predictions I had been hearing all week from Adam and Gibb that my car would certainly have been 'borrowed' over the Bank Holiday weekend for a night's joyriding, to my intense relief, it was still there on the quay, but liberally decorated by the Whitby gulls.

3

September - *Sophie Jayne*, Leigh-on-Sea

Fishing From The Cockle Capital

'Why do fishermen always start their day in the middle of the night?' was the thought going through my head as I looked for the *Sophie Jayne* at the Leigh-on-Sea quayside on a starlit night. At Leigh, the answer is obvious, the cockle fleet is so limited by the shallow channel, that they have to sail as and when the tide allows.

One by one wheelhouse lights were coming on along the quay, followed by engine after engine roaring into life before being throttled back to a growl. Steve Dell, owner of the *Sophie Jayne* crunched across the cockle shell gravel of the quay to the boat, where skipper Les Snell was preparing to start up.

I handed a few bags across to Steve, my bag of cameras, a pair of impressively sized cool boxes that I later found out contained their sandwiches for the day, my rather small sandwich box, and my other bag.

"What's in there?" Steve asked.

"That's my oilskins."

"What d'you want them for?"

"I thought I might need them on deck."

"You won't be needing them," he answered with a laugh.

Sophie Jayne has the berth at the end of the channel, and was the last to leave. As soon as there was enough water under the boat's keel, Les Snell began manoeuvring to get away from the quay, with part of the stern still sitting on the mud. Both Steve and I pushed at the pilings of the quay to shift the boat, and soon *Sophie Jayne* was underway.

"I expect Mason's been shoving the mud up here again," Les grumbled as the boat came free. Mason West, skipper of the *Paula Maree*, had just left his berth and his lights could be seen slipping away a short way ahead of us.

"We've tried to get Southend council to dredge the channel, but they just aren't interested in the fishing here," Steve explained. Each boat leaving the harbour has to go through these manoeuvres as soon as there is water under the keel, and this disturbs the bottom, pushing the mud further up to the top of the channel where the *Sophie Jayne* lies.

Les took the *Sophie Jayne* out through the narrow channel, steering to pass the end of Southend Pier, with the lights of the rest of the fleet ahead.

"There's a yacht in the channel, Les, if you want to keep an eye out for it," crackled across the VHF.

"They do this all the time," Les said. "These yachts come here and find they have to wait for the tide to get into Leigh, so they anchor up and go to sleep. The trouble is that they anchor right in the middle of the channel, instead of at the edge, and they don't always carry any lights."

As he spoke, the shadow of a sailing boat appeared in the gloom, and Les twitched the wheel to starboard to give it a wide berth. The anchored yacht was showing a masthead light, not visible to boats leaving Leigh, that could only be seen once the *Sophie Jayne* had left the yacht behind.

Several more warnings from skippers ahead came over the VHF, warning of yachts ahead, with or without lights, and a careful lookout for these had to kept until they had been left astern.

Once past Southend Pier, the way ahead was clearer, and Les set his course for a point close to the end of the Shoebury Boom.

While Steve and his father own the *Sophie Jayne*, they and Les work as a partnership, fishing for two days a week on grounds in the Thames Estuary. Les Snell has fished cockles from Leigh for practically all of his working life, starting as a youngster working from a small boat handraking cockles, with only his eyes, an alarm clock and a compass to navigate by.

He has lived and worked in Leigh-on-Sea all his life, apart from a short spell away as a steel erector, but returned to fishing.

"I even went up to Norfolk for a job once, but it didn't go as I wanted it to. Then I thought 'What am I doing here? I've got a family at home and there's work there,' so I came back to the cockles."

His forty years of fishing for cockles in the Thames have been mostly for the same company, and for thirty of those years the company has been owned by Steve Dell's family. Steve's father George, who had run a successful engineering business in Leigh for many years, bought the company in the 1960s, and has run it since as a family concern.

Cockle fishing from Leigh-on-Sea is a long established industry, going back certainly to the eighteenth century and possibly as far back as prehistoric times. The Thames Estuary has long had highly fertile fishing grounds, with shrimps, cockles, mussels and the oysters that were famous even in Roman times. The Thames is even thought to have been the birthplace of trawl fishing, something that is claimed by several different ports. But Thames fishing villages such as Barking certainly had sizable fishing fleets in the eighteenth and nineteenth centuries, before the focus of the expanding trawl industry moved out of the estuary and to ports closer to fishing grounds in the North Sea.

An indication of the antiquity of Leigh-on-Sea's cockle industry comes from Steve Dell, who explained that when the present day cockle sheds were being built some years ago to accommodate the processing plants, footings were dug six feet deep through nothing but compacted cockle shell and did not even reach into the soil that must be somewhere underneath.

Most of the Leigh boats now use fixed fishing gear, with a single solid pipe which carries the dredge on its end. Some of the boats still use the older gear, with a flexible pipe and the dredge towed from a warp. Fixed gear limits the boats to working in water shallower than the length of the pipe, about 25 feet, but the single rigid pipe is more reliable.

A suction pump draws cockles caught in the cage up through the main pipe into the rotating screen on deck and from there into the fishroom, while a second pump blows water out through a set of nozzles in front of the dredge. This loosens the cockles from the bottom, leaving them to be swept into the dredge's cage.

The normal layout for cockle boats is to have a main engine to propel the boat, with a heavy duty generator, often the same size as the main engine, used to power the boat's pumps, the winch used for handling the dredge, and the cranes that some use for landing their catches.

The present day cockle boats are the first generation of steel hulled boats to be built specifically for this kind of fishing, replacing the older wooden hulled boats that served the Leigh-on-Sea fishermen in the past.

"The old boats were built for handraking cockles, and for things like white weed fishing" Steve Dell said as we steamed out. "When the new fishing gear was introduced, the first suction dredges came in 1969 and were pioneered here with the White Fish Authority. The older boats just weren't built to carry it."

The power needed for suction dredging, combined with a need for increased carrying capacity, called for a new breed of boats, and almost all of the Thames cockle fleet, ten boats from Leigh and two from Whitstable in Kent, are now steel hulled purpose built boats.

"Because this is the first generation of boats, we don't really know how long they will last," Steve said. "But as long as we are only working two days a week, they should last a good few years yet."

Les Snell and Steve Dell of the *Sophie Jayne*.

Les at the *Sophie Jayne*'s wheel.

Steaming out, Steve has a few jobs to see to, such as checking the gilson wire for hoisting the dredge in and out of the water.

Another of the Leigh-on-Sea boats, Mason West's *Paula Maree* fishing on the same patch of ground.

Steve adjusting the dredge ready to shoot away.

Steve's old boat, *Katherine*, was sold to another local fisherman, and the *Sophie Jayne* was built in Newhaven in 1992, in anticipation of being able to fish more intensively. But the hopes of the Leigh-on-Sea fishermen were not realised, and the boat has never been able to fish at full capacity.

Sophie Jayne's fishroom can hold more than 1300 baskets of cockles, but quotas have been cut year after year, from 3000 baskets a week to 2000, and the current quota is for just 1000 baskets a week.

The fleet is also limited to fishing for two of three stipulated days in a week, and can only take 500 baskets on either of those days, which is less than half of the *Sophie Jayne*'s carrying capacity. Steve pointed out that the sides of the fishroom have been blanked off to limit its size, and the 500 basket threshold is marked on the bulkhead. When that is reached, it's time to go home.

Sophie Jayne steamed out onto the Maplin Sands that lie to the east of Leigh-on-Sea, and the heavy suction dredge was lowered over the side and into the water. The first cockles began to trickle through the screen and into the hold only a few moments after the dredge made contact with the seabed, while Les and Steve watched intently.

Steve explained that the process is very fast, and cockles from the dredge make their way through the 16mm gaps in the rotating screen just seconds after being sucked up from the dredge.

"What you see there is really what you are getting," he said.

Les watched carefully all the time, dividing his attention throughout the day between the wheelhouse and the rear window with its view over the hold, constantly watching the flow of shells into the fishroom. As soon as a greater than usual amount of broken shell or other debris began to show, he had an indication that the boat was off position. At intervals throughout the day, starting with a ladder to climb down, Steve made his way to the boat's fishroom to even out with a shovel the pile of cockles that collects under the chute. I could see why he was amused at my oilskins. He only needed to pull on a pair of wellies, and Les stayed in his shoes all day long.

"The cockles collect in channels, or Gutways as we call them." Les said. "The cleanest cockles are normally on the tops of flat grounds, but they are thicker in the guts. We try to keep to the sides of the gutways, as that's where they are clean. Any broken shell gets washed into the middles, and that's also where any shrapnel is."

Occasional lumps of blackened metal showed up amongst the cockles, and these were hooked out by Steve. The Maplin Sands have been a firing range for the army for decades, and there is an endless residue of the shells and bullets that have been tested there over the years.

Several times the tops of dummy shells fired during exercises came up with the cockles.

Later I heard stories of live shells being found, as well as bombs and mines left over from the war and even of adventurous fishermen who had retrieved the valuable copper bands from unexploded shells.

"The sands are always shifting," Steve said. "Things get covered up, and later the sands can shift to uncover them again." Les added that on some grounds round lead musket balls can be found with the catch, as well as larger balls that he feels could be from canisters of grapeshot from the days of sailing warships.

Steve went on to say that the lower area of the Maplin Sands is, strictly speaking, a completely closed area to any traffic, while on the upper area further from Leigh, boats can only pass through the area without stopping. "If they ever decided to enforce it, that would be the end of cockling in Leigh."

The Maplin Sands are the main area for the Thames cockle fleet, Les said. While there are a few other grounds, the Maplin Sands are the only areas where there are always cockles. Some areas have occasional patches of cockles, and there are other grounds that are only fished once in 20 years.

"We have worked as far out as the Shingles, but once you're out there you get some heavier seas. Inside the Estuary we have short, steep seas, which we can handle, but further out it rolls in straight off the North Sea and it's terrible trying to work in that." He added that when you are fishing in less than 20 feet of water, a 5 foot swell can be alarming, as well as dangerous when the depth is even less.

The Thames cockle fishermen have been through hard times in the past, especially following a time in the 1970s when a greater number of boats were fishing in the Estuary. The result is that since the regulating order for the Thames came into force in 1993, the number of licences has been kept to twelve by Kent and Essex Sea Fisheries Committee, which administers the fishery. Catches and fishing effort are strictly regulated and a 'two strikes and you're out' policy of enforcement exists.

A boat caught infringing the catch or time limits on two occasions will have its licence withdrawn and returned to the pool, but leaving the original holder ineligible to hold a licence again. Steve and the other fishermen feel that enforcing the regime of fishing days, in addition to a quota, is unnecessary.

"We are allowed to fish for two days a week out of Monday, Tuesday or Thursday, when we would like to see it open for two days out of four or even five. What happens is that if the weather is bad on a Monday and keeps the boats in, you know you've got to go on Tuesday and Thursday or lose out. It forces us to go when the weather isn't really fit for fishing. The quota should be enough to regulate the fishing effort without the specified days."

While the fishery is now regulated by the Kent and Essex Sea Fisheries Committee, until a few years ago it was administered by the Port of London Authority, and one of the cockle fishermen's main difficulties stems from the regulations put in force at that time.

"They stipulated that all the cockles caught had to be processed locally," Steve explained. "So we were all forced to either invest in processing plants or give up. Then two years later the rules were no longer valid, but we were left with this millstone around our necks. If we could just catch cockles and send them away for processing, we'd be quids in."

In the past there have been years when the cockles in the Thames were severely overfished, with boats coming from outside the Thames, and the result is the present strict regulation of the fishery.

"We've seen what can happen, and we don't want it to happen again," Les commented. "We have had some really good years," Steve added. "But there are still no rich cockle fishermen. The good years see you through the worst ones, and it evens itself out over a period of time." Limited to only half of the year, all of the boats are tied up from the end of the year until the season reopens in June. This leaves them inactive for six months with no other fishery they are able to pursue, a long time for a boat to be tied up with no income.

After a most of the morning on the Maplin Sands, Les decided to shift to other grounds to finish the day. The dredge was lifted and the generator shut down as he steamed the *Sophie Jayne* south to the Burrows. Here there were already several boats at work, and more could be seen steaming southwards behind us.

The cockles on the Burrows flowed faster into the *Sophie Jayne*'s hold, and Steve's trips with the shovel to even them out became more frequent. Once Les found a patch he was happy with, the wheel went hard over, and he circled tightly over it, while the other boats working on the same grounds were doing exactly the same over a half mile area of ground, all going around in tight circles strung out in a line along the same channel.

With the 500 mark on the bulkhead reached, the dredge was finally lifted and the *Sophie Jayne* steamed back towards Leigh-on-Sea. Tea was made on the stove in the wheelhouse and the sandwiches boxes came out for the hour's steam homewards.

No need for oilskins - as the cockles roll down the chute into the hold, all Steve has to do is to even them out when they start to pile up.

Steve clears the cage of the cockle dredge while steaming to other grounds.

Les brings *Sophie Jayne* round in a tight circle and drops the dredge back into the water.

With the tide rising, the channel up to the quay at Leigh-on-Sea still isn't deep enough for the boat to get through. A queue of boats waits for *Katherine*, still sitting on the mud.

A grab and a digger are used to land the cockles and take them the few yards to the processing plant.

A handful of freshly caught, freshly cooked cockles.

With Southend Pier one side and Leigh-on-Sea on the other, the cockle fleet tied up to a mooring to wait the three hours for the tide to rise. While some of the crews gathered on the deck of one boat to yarn the afternoon away with a few cans of beer, others went below to catch up on a few hours sleep.

Later that afternoon the sun was dropping when the moorings were slipped and the boats began to make their way in. With the trippers watching from a few yards away on the beach, and with children swimming a few yards away in the channel, the row of boats crawled into Leigh through a channel so narrow and winding that it was hard to believe that Les had taken the *Sophie Jayne* out through it in the dark that morning. Steaming in behind *Katherine* and ahead of *Paula Maree*, Les guided *Sophie Jayne* through the twists until the *Katherine*, a few yards ahead, came to a gentle but firm halt on the mud of the bottom of the channel. There was nothing for it but to wait for the tide to rise a little more, until the water was deep enough for *Katherine* to float free again. Once past, Les inched *Sophie Jayne* ahead to the top of the channel, past *Paula Maree* and the *Solway Harvester*, already tied up at their berths and with their day's catches on their way up to be processed.

Once *Sophie Jayne* was at the quayside, a grab was used to crane the cockles ashore and into the waiting scoop of a digger. Landing does not take long, and it also has to be quick to feed the cookers ashore that were already waiting for the catch.

"The quicker we get them cooked, the better the yield," Steve explained. "A basket of cockles should yield a gallon of meat, but the longer they are kept the further the yield falls. If it's a hot day the cockles caught at the start of the trip can sometimes drop to a yield of half a gallon a basket."

The cooked cockles that Steve and Les land are exported to Holland, and the lorry was already there waiting to pick up the day's catch.

"A lot of people look at what we are doing here and think we are earning a fortune," Steve said. "But these processing plants ashore are very expensive to run. One of them has a bigger water bill than Southend hospital," he added.

"People don't always see the industry ashore. We've been saddled with that and we'll have to stick with it," he said, and commented that there are more than 100 jobs ashore linked to Leigh-on-Sea's cockle fleet.

"What is worrying us here is that legislation as it stands will not allow us an increase in effort when stocks recover. When the cockle stocks improve, they are at liberty to issue new licences instead of allowing established fishermen to increase their effort."

65

He said that there have been applications for licences from boats elsewhere in the country to operate in the Thames. At the same time, the local fishermen are working two days a week for half the year, with all of the shore staff involved in processing now limited to working part time.

"We have done the hard work, and there is the possibility that they could give it all away. We feel that we should be able to go back to full employment. We want to see our own people with proper jobs again before any more licences can be issued. The truth is that there isn't enough to go round. But we were here first and we feel that we're the ones who ought to be entitled to it."

Silhouetted against the early morning sun, Paul and Ken haul the first day's nets.

Deckhand Ken at *Sandra's* net hauler brings another of the gillnets aboard into a heap on the deck.

David Stevens on the *Crystal Sea* uses an iron bar to take a turn out of one of the sweeplines.

David picks fish from the meshes of the *Crystal Sea's* codend.

David and Tuc at the stern, watching the trawl come to the surface.

Shooting away *Carisanne's* trawl for the first haul of the trip.

A bag of fish is hauled aboard *Carisanne* to be emptied into the fish pound.

Fish in the pounds on board *Carisanne*.

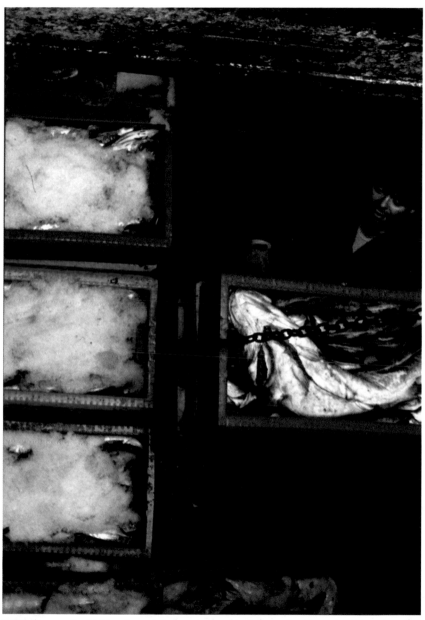

Gibb the cook shifting boxes into position under the hatch to be lifted out and swung onto the quay at Scarborough.

Clipping in one of the doors on board *Carisanne*.

Courage's crew with the purse seine neatly stacked back in the net bin.

George West in *Courage's* wheelhouse.

James Alexander at the triplex watches as the purse seine is hauled.

4

October - *Courage*, Fraserburgh

The Art Of Purse Seining

At the far end of the Broch's harbour, with spray coming over the tops of the breakwaters, I found George West's *Courage* tied up among a group of other pelagic boats. It was late on a windy night when I arrived in Fraserburgh, not looking forward to sailing into a northerly force nine. To my relief, George West had postponed departure for a day, allowing the weather to drop and me to look around the harbour and granite village of Fraserburgh.

Over the next day, the boats began to leave harbour one by one. *Daystar* and *Christina S* steamed out into the heaving seas past the breakwater that morning, and later in the day *Grateful* and *Convallaria* headed out as well, pitching heavily into the long, rolling waves. I was not entirely unhappy that George West had put out off sailing until that night. Throughout the day the wind had continued to blow hard, but towards evening the weather had begun to die away. Some of the larger whitefish trawlers had started to make their way out of the harbour as well, when a hammering on the dog catches on one of the outside doors was the first indication that some of *Courage*'s crew were arriving on board.

A face appeared around the corner of the cabin door. "Hullo, so you're the writer. Well, you've chosen a fine night for it," he said, and was gone.

I had already made myself comfortable in the upper bunk of one of the cabins down below, sharing with James Alexander, *Courage*'s second skipper, who did his best to hide his concern for the decor of his cabin.

"Have you been to sea before?" he asked first, appearing to be satisfied when I said that I had.

"Well, there's the toilets just down there," he said, pointing along the passageway. "Just in case..."

The crew introduced themselves one by one, each one of them speaking carefully, and slipping back into doric, the north east of Scotland dialect, as the conversation included someone else.

The ship came to life rapidly, and lights all over the vessel flickered off and on again as the main engine rumbled into life. Stores for the trip, including bags of potatoes, trays of vegetables, boxes of biscuits and bread, and crates of milk and fruit juice were handed inside and down to the cook's store in the galley, where Ian the cook could hardly put things away fast enough. Crewmen bustled back and forth, and in the area behind the galley some of the crew were pulling on oilskin trousers and coats ready for the deck. Outside, with the wind still blowing hard enough to sting cheeks, the crew made their way onto the deck to cast off the ropes, coiling them away carefully.

George eased *Courage* away from the quay, squeezing with what seemed to be inches to spare through the narrow channel to the outer harbour and out into the channel leaving Fraserburgh harbour for the open sea. Passing the end of the breakwater and into the full force of the white flecked waves, *Courage* began to roll heavily in the darkness, but behaved better as soon as the shallow water had been cleared. George explained that all of the RSW (refrigerated sea water) tanks had been filled with water and pressed up. "It's not so good for the stability, but it's more comfortable."

Courage's engine room is aft, and all of the accommodation is in the stern and in the two levels of the superstructure below the wheelhouse. Apart from the forecastle, the rest of the 201 feet of *Courage*'s length consists of the six RSW tanks that are used to keep catches fresh, and which could in theory hold 900 tonnes of chilled fish if filled to capacity.

A few years ago George West and his family were looking to replace one of their two aging purser/trawlers, and brought the *Azalea* to Fraserburgh as the *Courage*.

Courage was built in Norway twenty years ago, as a purse seiner for owners in Shetland. She was lengthened amidships some years later to increase carrying capacity, and later lengthened still further at the stern to fit trawl drums and a stern gantry for pelagic trawling as half of a pair team.

Courage steamed through an uncomfortable night, with wind and sea buffeting the port side as we headed north east into the last gasps of the strong northerly wind. Early the following morning the wind had died away to a stiff breeze, with whitecaps still showing but not enough to make life on a 200 foot boat uncomfortable.

"We're heading for the Beryl oilfield," George West said in the morning, sitting high up in *Courage*'s wheelhouse with the low autumn sun shining on a speckled sea. These are grounds not far from the Norwegian sector of the North Sea, where he expected to find enough mackerel to finish what was left of the boat's quota for the year. "A bit of bad weather can bring them up to the surface. They seem to concentrate behind it as the weather improves," George explained.

The herring quota had been finished a few weeks before, and most of *Courage*'s mackerel quota had already been caught at the beginning of the year, leaving only a few hundred tonnes to be caught by the *Courage* and the *Prowess*, skippered by George's brother David.

With little remaining of *Courage*'s quota, the emphasis would be on landing fish to the highest bidder, most likely a Norwegian processing factory.

"The fish is auctioned at sea," George said. "We send a message with what we have on board, the amount and the size of the fish, and the factories bid for it. We can specify what area we want to land in, but the bigger the area specified, the more competition there is and the more chance of a higher price."

The auction is run by one of the Norwegian fishermen's associations, primarily for the Norwegian fleet, but Scottish, Irish, Shetland and Danish boats all use it to sell their fish to processing factories in Norway. The auction takes place several times a day, and a reply normally comes back fairly quickly from whatever factory has bid successfully for the fish.

That afternoon *Courage* was on the fishing grounds, and George West in the wheelhouse was concentrating on the sonar screens in front of him, two high frequency sets, and a low frequency sonar. The low frequency sonar has a longer range, but does not give such clear marks. "We use it a lot for herring, but it's not so good for mackerel as they have much smaller swim bladders that don't give such a strong echo."

George concentrated constantly, and his attention never strayed far from the sonar screens directly in front of him. As other members of the crew made their way up to the wheelhouse, standing quietly at the back, or staring out of the windows at the distant oil rigs, everyone's eyes sooner or later came to rest on the sonar screens, waiting for a mark to appear between the two side lobe marks that show the extent of the sonar's 180° field of view.

By this time, we had been on the fishing grounds for only a few hours, and the rest of the fleet had been searching for marks without any success for a day and a night.

All 201 feet of the *Courage* tied up at the quayside by the West Fish plant in Ålesund.

Skipper Geoge West.

"Awa' the dahn boys." George West sounds the whistle and deckhand Ali
Maitland lets go the drogue to shoot the purse seine away.

"The other boats are all about 20 miles north of us," George said and pointed to the printer where there were messages from other pursers and trawlers passed over the Inmarsat satellite system, the only way of sending confidential messages at sea.

"Puckle marks here. Nae great," one message read.

A mark that appeared on the sonar showed that something was to be found, and George cruised slowly around it several times. "They're mackerel all right," he said, pointing to the echo sounder screen as he brought *Courage* close to the shoal. "They're showing up there on the high frequency but not on the low frequency side of the screen."

The crew were already busy on deck, switching over to the purse seine gear from the pair trawl setup. "I'm a purse seine man, but the boys don't like it," George said with a smile. "Too much work. They prefer trawling. When you're trawling you always get something after four hours towing, but with the seine there's always the chance that there's no fish in there."

He continued to follow the mark on the sonar screen, not letting his attention wander from it for more than a few moments at a time. "It's going northwards," he said, indicating the readout in a corner of the screen that showed the course and speed of the shoal. "The ones who found some mackerel further north all said that they were swimming north as well."

Courage's track relative to the shoal could be seen on the sonar screen as George had circled it warily. With the fishing gear ready to shoot, George guided *Courage* into position to shoot away the seine in the path of the mackerel, sounding a series of short blasts on the whistle to tell the crew aft to let the dahn buoy at the end of the seine go. Soon the lead weights on the footrope of the net could be heard rattling over the side of the big net bin as the gear was paid away. At the same time the heavy steel purse rings that close the bottom edge of the net shot off the shooting bar one by one, each in a cloud of rust flakes, as George brought *Courage* around in a ring to close the circle around the fish.

Down on the deck, and directly below the wheelhouse window, deckhand Richard Strachan counted the rings away, shouting above the din, to let George and first mate Alistair Gibson know how far the net had been shot.

"Three. Two. Gone!" Richard yelled as the last few rings shot off the bar, loud enough to be heard in the wheelhouse over the noise of the engine, and the gear rattling into the sea.

Once the last ring had gone, Stanley May at the winch in front of the wheelhouse began to let the wedge wire pay away from the boat, and James, with his beloved Celtic woolly hat pulled down over his ears against the chill, took his place at the triplex winch, used for hauling the massive seine back on board.

"You'd better be careful where you stand," he warned me. "This is the wettest place on the boat."

As he spoke, water slopped through the scupper around our ankles.

"You're now going to see an exercise in the art of fuck-ups. Trawling's much better than this. Better for us, anyway. Not better for him," another of the crew said, waving an arm towards the wheelhouse.

With the circle complete, hopefully with the shoal inside, Stan at the winch began to bring in the wedge wire, responding to shouted instructions from the wheelhouse window above to haul or stop the winch.

Eventually the end appeared in the hatch at the side, and James quickly shackled a heavy rope into it, leading up through the triplex. Stan slacked away the wedge wire, and the strain was taken on the rope, leading up through the three heavy rollers of the triplex, with Richard and Joe Cardno in the net bin behind hanging on the rope to start bringing the end of the net through.

Soon the end of the net appeared, first the big mesh in the wedge of the seine. This part of the net can be larger mesh, as this is not needed to contain fish, rather to frighten them away. The whole of the top of the net, the corkline, is lined with yellow floats, and these squeal as if in pain as they pass through the triplex rollers, while the lead line at the bottom the seine passes through easily. One man stacks the corkline carefully at the far end of the big net bin, while another painstakingly stacks and arranges the heavy lead line in neat rows so that it can be shot safely next time.

As the process continued, more and more of the crew made their way aft, and eventually everyone on board, with the exception of James at the triplex and the skipper in the wheelhouse, was helping stack the seine, taking armfuls of the heavy nylon net and dropping folds of it into the right places ready to be shot away again.

This is backbreaking work for the crew, and even Ian the cook and Johnny and Martin the two engineers take part in this, manhandling the heavy net with its tiny meshes. Oilskins are essential as water cascades constantly onto their heads from the net as it passes through the roller of the netstacker over their heads.

Courage's purse seine weighs around 20 tonnes, and measures 360 fathoms along the corkline. It is 95 fathoms deep, but the net is hung by a half, and that depth would be impossible to reach. "Realistically we can fish down to about 75 fathoms," George told me later. "But fishing that deep it takes a long time to sink, it takes longer to shoot and the more accurate you have to be in shooting."

The deeper the shot, and the longer the leadline of the net takes to sink, the greater the opportunity for the fish to become aware of their danger and swim away before the seine is pursed around them. "You have to allow for tide and wind," George went on to explain. "As well as the movement of the fish. Normally you'll find that the fish are moving in a direction that is the worst one there could be for wind and tide."

As the net is pursed, the steel purse rings collect on the purse wire forward where the end of the net is tied up. As the length of the seine is brought aboard through the triplex, the rings follow it one by one, and it is part of James' job to keep an eye on them, snapping them off as they get close to the block, closing the rings again and dropping them onto the net to go through the triplex with the net. Every minute or so there is a clang as a purse ring is pulled through the triplex and lands on the metal chute leading up to the netstacker directly above the net bin.

Each purse ring threatens to crack a head as it comes tumbling through with the net, so hard hats in the net bin are a must. Ian the cook takes each purse ring as it comes through, threading them back onto the shooting bar ready to go again.

"He seems quite excited," gasped one of the deck crew with half the net brought aboard, meaning George in the wheelhouse far above. "So I suppose there might be something in it this time."

George called from the wheelhouse down to the deck frequently to check progress, and kept a constant eye on the triplex winch where James the second mate was controlling the hauling operations. He later said that recently a man was killed on another boat after being caught up in the winch and pulled through with the net. Prominent on the dashboard on the starboard side of the wheelhouse is a red stop button, which brings the hydraulics to an immediate halt if punched.

Hauling the seine is a long job, and it was not until most of the net had been hauled that the first fish began to show themselves, shining mackerel caught in bights of the net right under the triplex winch, or 'walking' on their tails across the pool of water inside the decreasing ring of the purse seine.

It took the best part of an hour to bring most of the net on board, and for the bag of the seine to be alongside. Several of the crew made their way forward and struggled to clip the heavy rubber hoses, more than a foot in diameter, together using big aluminium clips. Once the hose was manhandled into position, the big pump was suspended from the ship's crane and dropped over the side into the net. As the pumps started up, water sprayed from every join in the hoses and seconds later the first glittering mackerel, shivering and shining, began to come through the

Deckhand Joe Cardno watches as the gear is shot away from the big net bin at *Courage*'s stern.

Richard Strachan shouts out to the wheelhouse to let the skipper know how much of the net has been shot.

Waiting to start pursing.

James Alexander Clipping the wedge into the leader rope to start hauling the purse seine on board.

separator on the hatch to fall along the chute and into the tanks forward. A couple of basketfuls of fish were taken out and carried forward to the weighing station under the whaleback.

"Just goin' to get myself a tickler first," David 'Tigger' Lyon said, extracting a baccy tin and a couple of ready rolled rollups from an inside pocket before slapping one mackerel after another onto the electronic scales, knocking their heads against the edge of a basket to ensure that they lay still to be weighed.

"650 grammes..., 350 grammes..., That's a fine mackerel, 800 grammes...," until three basketfuls had been weighed and the printer chattered a readout showing the average weights of the fish.

As Tigger was weighing the samples, George came down from the wheelhouse to have a look for himself, taking a couple of the glittering fish and filleting them quickly. Norwegian processors are particular about quality, and require as much information as possible before they bid for fish that is still in a fishing vessel's tanks at sea, and the condition of the fish and the type of feed in the stomachs of the fish can make a big difference in quality, and in price.

In the auction system run by the Norwegians, each vessel can declare the amount of fish caught, its condition, where it was caught, and whether it was caught in a purse seine or a trawl. There is also the option of specifying a preferred landing area, so only fish processing plants inside that area will bid for the fish.

The crew's mood had lightened immediately it was clear that there was a reasonable amount of fish in the net, and the laughter and jokes snapped back and forth across the deck

Down on *Courage*'s deck, with the fish steadily pouring into the tanks, very welcome hot coffee was handed round in plastic cups, and the word came that George was planning to take some fish from partner vessel *Prowess*, skippered by his brother David, fishing a few miles further north.

"That'll give you some good pictures when you've got the two boats side by side," James said. "Then it looks like we'll be going to Norway. Don't you worry, we'll buy you a pint when we get there."

Half an hour later, with the fish on board and the crew finishing off getting the gear ready for shooting again, there was a change of plan. Instead of pumping fish from *Prowess*' nets, George decided to try for another shot of mackerel. The crew made themselves tea or coffee, knocked themselves together hasty sandwiches, or sat in the TV room for a smoke. This was the first time for four hours that they had been able to take their boots and oilskins off.

"How long until the next one?"

"Could be 10 minutes. Could be two hours," James said.

"Or it could be two days," added mate Alistair Gibson.

In the wheelhouse George pointed to a smallish mark on the sonar screen that he had been circling and watching, carefully evaluating its size, course and density.

All around the *Courage* a sizable fleet of pursers and trawlers had congregated.

"The jungle grapevine is incredible," George said without looking up from the sonar. "I told one person about fish, and all these boats have come down from the north. All boats from Fraserburgh and Peterhead."

A few miles away was a massive offshore oil vessel, constantly burning off gas from the top of a pipe at its stern. More oil rigs could be seen in the distance, and a guard boat from the rig was there to keep fishing boats away from the oil installations.

George's attention remained constantly on the sonars in front of the skipper's chair, with a conversation going on over the VHF in a dialect so strong that an outsider could only catch two words in three.

"We were too far ahead last time, and it was touch and go," George said. "We had to wait for a while for the fish to swim up into the net."

"Away the dahn boys. Away the dahn," George murmured into the ship's intercom system so that his words could be heard everywhere on board. This is the signal to get ready to shoot, and George explained that the expression has remained in use, even though dahn buoys have not been used to mark the end of the seine for years.

The crew were waiting on deck for the word to let the dahn go, and as George gave a couple of blasts on the whistle to shoot, Alistair the mate stood at the wheelhouse window to relay progress on the deck. This time there was a delay of only a few seconds between the whistle blasts and the dahn and the end of the net being shot away.

At last it began to clatter away over the stern as George brought *Courage* round to head off the shoal. The net was shot, and the ring closed, but among the purse rings there was something wrong, and the net had clearly been snagged during shooting.

"If there's any damage there, it could put us out of action for the rest of the night," George said in worried tones. "You can get in some terrible situations with a purse," he explained, and added that serious damage can result in twenty four hours just getting the net on board, followed by days of mending on the quay. The crew are paid a share of the catch, and while working on the gear they are not earning anything.

The slow process of hauling the seine continued, with the same backbreaking work for the crew in the net bin, regardless of how much fish there is in the net. By now it was getting on towards evening with darkness about to fall. A squat guard boat from one of the oil rigs took up station a boat's length from *Courage*'s port side, as we were clearly getting too close to one of the exclusion zones for his liking. As the net was finally brought alongside, it was clear that this shot had been for nothing and the very few fish in the net were released.

"We should have taken that fish from the *Prowess*," George said with the benefit of hindsight. The first shot of fish, guessed to be close to 100 tonnes, was put on the auction, and George set course for Norway as the crew began the laborious task of mending the torn net. Fortunately the damage was relatively small, and close to the end of the seine, making it fairly easily accessible. It was fully dark by the time they finished lacing the fine meshed net together and started to make their way inside for the evening meal. News came through that a factory in Måløy had bid for the fish, and George expected to be there the following afternoon.

"Are you going to fly home from here, or do you want to come out with us again?" George asked on the steam to Måløy. "It looks like we'll be doing another trip."

"I'll stay with you if that's all right."

"That's no problem. You're very welcome to stay."

On the long steam to Måløy the crew were able to take things easy. Everyone appeared showered and shaved in *Courage*'s long messroom with its four wide tables for the meal at midday, and by early afternoon *Courage* was steaming in perfect weather parallel to the sunlit Norwegian coast, rocky and tree lined, but still free of the snow that can make this craggy coast such an awe inspiring sight in winter.

In the wheelhouse George prepared to steam into Nordfjord to get to Måløy, a small town which has four processing companies operating plants to handle pelagic fish. *Fertile* was ahead of us, and was sighted a short way from Måløy steaming in under the bridge that spans the fjord with a single graceful sweep. Steaming into Måløy, the crew pointed out the different factories, each with one or more fishing vessels tied up alongside. *Fertile* steamed further along the fjord to the Domstein factory, the largest in Måløy, while a Norwegian purser was pumping fish ashore to another plant a few yards from *Courage*'s berth at the Emy Fish processing factory. A Shetland purser followed us in to Måløy, heading for the bigger plant further along the fjord.

Emy Fish is one of the smaller processors. Much of the workforce appeared at the doors to take a look at the foreign purser, every one of them wearing the Norwegian national dress of boiler suit and baseball cap with the company logo. As I snapped off pictures of the crew tying *Courage* up, some of them did their best to convince me that the ubiquitous 'Lensing Forbut' signs, prohibiting pumping out bilges in harbour, actually forbid photography.

Once the ropes were made fast, the crane on board was started and used to lift up the landing box, into which *Courage*'s fish were to be pumped and transferred straight to the factory.

"These deep water berths are the Norwegian processors' single biggest asset," George said later. Apart from a factory in Shetland with a similar berth where pursers can tie up to land their fish directly into a factory, landing pelagic fish in Scottish ports is a laborious process that means transporting fish in tubs and on lorries, with the fish losing some of its quality every time it is handled.

Inside the plant there was a complete contrast to the dilapidated exterior of the building. Everything was scrubbed and spotless, with gleaming stainless steel equipment already grading the fish into four sizes. The girls at the graders deftly check the weights of the fish as they pass along a series of conveyors to weighing and packing stations, while holding non-stop conversations despite the rattle of machinery.

Whenever possible this plant processes fish for export to Japan, a market which appreciates quality and is prepared to pay for it, but which makes stringent requirements on quality and quality control. A Japanese inspector was at the plant, constantly taking samples of fish, and examining each one for colour and freshness. This is the man who makes the decision on whether or not the fish will be suitable for Japanese consumers and his thumbs up sign is all important. A thumbs down means that fish will have to be processed for less lucrative markets such as Russia or eastern Europe, or worse still, that the fishing boat will be sent over the fjord to the local fishmeal factory to land its catch for processing into meal and eventually used as cattle or fish food, and where the price is much lower than it is for human consumption.

At the Emy Fish plant empty cartons roll along overhead conveyors to the weighing stations, each of which spits out a box full of gleaming mackerel every few seconds. Everything in the factory area is immaculately hygienic and the fish are treated like royalty on their journey to the deep freezers. At the final stage of the process, each box has a lining of plastic sheet, which the factory girls fold lovingly over before closing the cardboard flaps and shoving the boxes along the conveyor to be strapped and taken to the freezers.

The large mesh wedge is the first part of the big purse seine to come through the rollers of the triplex winch.

Steaming under the bridge into Måløy for the first landing of the trip.

The factory girls at the Emy Fish plant are packing *Courage*'s fish wthin a few minutes of it being pumped ashore.

An inspector representing the buyers in Japan fillets fish after fish to check the quality. He has the final word on whether the fish is good enough for the Japanese market.

The whole process takes a matter of minutes, and the plant's owner, a serious young Norwegian businessman, also dressed in the uniform of boiler suit and cap, explained that only ten minutes pass between the fish coming out of the *Courage*'s tanks and being put into the freezers.

Emy Fish is a young company, run by Magnus Strand and his brother who also have a salmon export business. The processing plant is the old Domstein factory, sold to the brothers when that company moved to new premises on the other side of the fjord, where another Scottish vessel could be seen discharging its catch of mackerel.

"You can be very proud of the quality of your fish today," Magnus Strand told George West over coffee in the company's office while the fish was being pumped ashore and the production line on the floor below was working at full tilt. He explained what he had been looking for in the auction. "The fish should be only one shot and it should be pursed mackerel," he said, and added that another Scottish boat's catch of trawl caught mackerel had been downgraded earlier that day and processed for other markets, and bought at a lower price than he could offer for fish good enough for Japan.

It was clear that he had felt he was taking a risk on bidding for *Courage*'s fish, and was highly relieved that his gamble had paid off. "I have made a lot of money on *Courage*, and I only bid *Courage*'s fish at the auction. I could see that it was pursed fish and only one shot, and I thought that this was the least risky one to bring into Norway."

"It is still too early in the year for trawled mackerel, and it is very difficult to get the best quality fish. But I knew your boat already and was sure that I would get the same quality again. The distance between the shot and the port is important to get the best quality. It's important to know the vessel and the people, and I had dealt with *Courage* before."

During the trip, Tigger had developed a bad toothache on the way out from Fraserburgh, with an abscess under an infected tooth. Clearly in some pain, and with the side of his face swollen 'like a bap', he had lasted the trip with painkillers from the ship's medical stores.

As the fish were pumped ashore, he waited for the promised dentist's appointment in Måløy.

"How's your teeth, Tigger?" George asked as the three of us stepped ashore into the factory.

"Nae great. And it's interfering with my eating."

"Well, we can't have that."

In the Emy Fish offices, Magnus Strand made a quick call to arrange an appointment.

"The dentist can see you at seven o'clock. He's the same dentist that I go to."

George looked at his watch.

"That's six our time. Do you want to wait on board until then, Davie?"

"Aye, I will that," Tigger replied with relief in his voice. "I'll come back at six, then."

Part of the problem for the foreign boats landing to processors in Norway at this time of the year is that Norwegian waters, where most of the mackerel are to be found, are closed to them. There is competition with the Norwegian pursers, who have shorter distances to run to port to discharge, and who have much wider grounds to fish on.

"It is most important for us that we catch all of our quota," George West explained. Towards the end of the year mackerel are delicate and require very careful handling, but they have to be caught when they are there.

"If Norwegian waters were open to us it would be a lot easier for us to come to Norway with small shots of fish. But we have to catch our quota when it's there. We can't afford not to."

From the talk between George and Magnus over frequently refilled cups of coffee in the Emy Fish offices, it is clear that the business can be as risky for the buyer as it could be for George. Reputations are vital, as the pelagic business is centred around the auctions at sea, and buyers have no choice but to bid for fish without having seen them for themselves.

"If I bid for three or four boats' catch, I could get them all, and then I would have to take them all as well," Magnus Strand explained. "Normally I bid for a maximum of 200 tonnes, and would most probably get one or two vessels in a day."

The reputations of the boats and their skippers plays an important part in the process. George later told me that a new vessel entering the market will almost invariably get only low prices for its fish until a good enough reputation has been built up for the buyers to trust the skipper's word on the quality of his catch.

Courage sailed from Måløy in darkness, steaming out under the big bridge with George concentrating on the radar screen in front of him and the plotter showing all the lights and buoys in the passage out of the fjord.

On deck the crew were putting away all the mooring ropes and the landing gear, with the big hopper dropped back down on its telescoping legs and the pump hoses ready for fishing again. Engineer Martin Smart was freezing water again, with the forward tanks each holding 50 tonnes of sea water gradually being chilled down to just below freezing point. This means that fish pumped aboard are dropped straight into chilled water to keep them in peak condition for the long steam to shore.

When steaming, George leaves the wheelhouse to the rest of the crew, who are organised into watches. Everyone takes a steaming watch for a few hours, keeping an eye on the radar and peering into the gloom at night, keeping the little ship icon on the plotter close to the track set by George to where he wants the ship taken. There is no shortage of qualified men on board. For a boat that requires three tickets, there are four full skipper's tickets on board, and three mate's tickets among the crew, the result of having a nautical college on their doorstep in Fraserburgh. Steaming back to the fishing grounds, the crew caught up on their sleep, read in their bunks or watched the TV (Norwegian television with no sound) until the picture began to fade, after which the stock of videos rented for the trip came into use. Some of the crew also brought their own videos, bringing them up from cabins below when the rented tapes had all been watched again and again.

Between videos, two meals a day appeared on the galley table. "I used to do three meals," Ian explained. "But not everyone turned out for every meal, and I was throwing away food. It was a waste and we went back to two meals a day."

There is always an evening meal, and either breakfast or a midday meal, depending on working hours. In between, the crew have access to the stores and the fridge, and sandwiches and microwaved snacks can always be thrown together.

Breakfast is a heavy meal of bacon, eggs, sausages and black pudding, preceded by porridge, although only Stanley salts his porridge. Everyone else spoons golden syrup into bowls of porridge, and some add a generous spoonful of sugar on top of that.

"This is a pretty good berth," one of the crew said in the TV room as we steamed back towards the fishing grounds. "There's nothing illegal goes on here, we don't do black fish, so the money isn't as good as it can be on some boats. On some of the bigger boats it can be different, so I'm not surprised it took you a while to find someone to take you out. They get greedier all the time, and some of them treat their crews like shit. There were even a couple of boats not long ago that couldn't sail because they couldn't get a crew to go on them."

Someone else chimed in to say that earnings are reasonable, from £22,000 for a reasonable year to as much as £41,000 for a record year, but the bulk of the money is in the spring mackerel season.

"If you don't get anything in January, February and March, you've had it for the year."

Some of the crew would clearly be happier if there were some black fish landed to boost their earnings, and there are stories bandied about of the impressive figures quoted for crew shares on boats that do go in for landing illegal fish.

As is the nature of fishermen everywhere when the talk turns to money, not all of the crew are completely satisfied with their lot, seeing times as getting harder. "It used to be half for the boat and half for the boys, but it's not like that any more. They just do the same as the others," one of them said, pointing upwards to indicate the wheelhouse.

"We're longer at sea with the mackerel now. Ten years ago we would be at home every weekend, but you never see that now."

"The physical side of it has changed as well. It's a lot easier now," James said. Now that catches are normally pumped ashore, there is no longer the need to land and box hundreds of tonnes of fish on the quayside at the end of a trip.

"25 boxes was a tonne, so 16 tonnes was 400 boxes," Richard said. "You used to have to spend four or five hours at the end of a trip boxing fish and stacking it on lorries. It was a total nightmare."

"Twenty-four lorries was a good landing," another of the crew added. "Sometimes they'd even be meat lorries, still with the meat hooks hanging in them."

"And this is a man who has landed about a million boxes of fish," James said, slapping Stanley's knee. "It's not as physically demanding as it was, it's just that black bastard up there," he added, meaning the 20 tonne weight of the purse seine.

"There's too much time away from home, and in your spare time you have you can only read and watch TV. You can't do anything else. My advice to any young school leaver would be 'forget it. You only have one life, use it well. If there was anything else I could do, I'd do it. If I could step into a job ashore, I would.'"

"I quite enjoy it, to be honest with you," commented ship's cook Ian Whyte, who trained and worked as a chef ashore for many years before trying his hand at fishing.

"But it's not the same for you," came the quick reply. "You've got a different point of view to us."

"But I'd worked ashore, and I wasn't happy with it," Ian admitted.

James told me that he had intended to join the navy to train as a helicopter pilot on leaving school, and had stayed on at school to sit his higher exams. His naval ambitions were thwarted by a lazy eye, and he found himself watching his friends leaving school and going fishing.

James unclipping one of the heavy purse rings from the purse wire.

David 'Tigger' Lyon. Stacking the
seine is a long and backbreaking task.

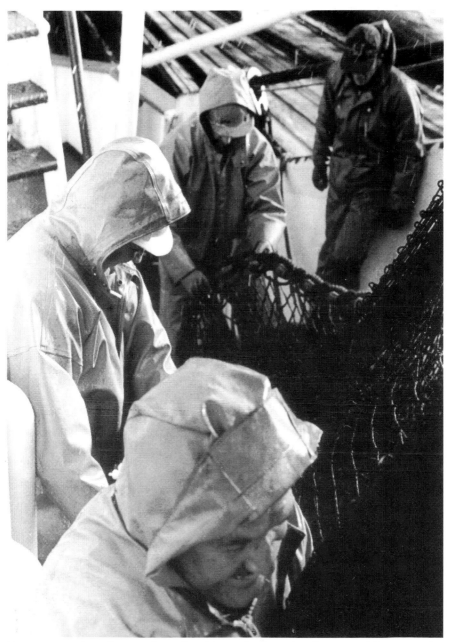

Everyone on board apart from the skipper in the wheelhouse and James at the triplex stacks the net, dripped on all the time with water from the net.

"I saw my friends making money and I thought I'd better get some as well. When I started we were making much more than people ashore, but their wages are catching up and now there are shore jobs making just as much money as we are."

One of the older crewmen made the point that 24 years ago herring were making £100 a tonne. "But today we are averaging £90 a tonne. It speaks for itself. It's hardly worth going to sea any more."

Many of them see themselves as tied to the fishing industry, with few alternatives available either ashore or at sea. "I'd like to go to the offshore boats, like a lot of them did," another of the deckhands says. "But they're looking for younger men in their twenties now, and I'm past that, so I'm stuck with fishing."

"The only reason I'm still here is that George is such a good man to work for," another chimed in. "If it wasn't for that, I'd be long gone."

"Aye, he's a fine guy," another voice added. "You couldn't ask for a finer guy to work for. You never hear him. He's so laid back that sometimes you want to go up there and gee him up a bit."

"The job has its good sides as well," James said. "When you're at home your time's your own."

"We'll have a week at least at home now after this trip," Tigger said." My kids are on tattie holidays now, so I'll have a week with them. There'll be work to do on the gear, but it's still a week ashore and in my own bed every night."

Seeing me with my notebook open, Tigger nodded his head to indicate me.

"We'd all better buy this book when it comes out, and see which of us is still going to have a job."

With that the conversation turned to speculation on how long the stopover would be likely to last.

"I've been at home for bonfire night every year since I started here," another voice added.

"Now it'll be a panic to get ready for the sprats," someone else commented. "That net's got to come off and we'll put the sprat net on. That takes five or six hours. Then the big trawl's got to come off that drum and the other trawl goes on there. Should be two days' work and a few days at home."

"We did well on the sprats last year. The price was high in Denmark, but it'll be lower this year. Last year it was that cold that the harbour in Esbjerg was frozen and two mile out the sea was still ice."

After the sprat season in the North Sea, *Courage*'s crew can expect to be back in Fraserburgh for the rest of the year, before the mackerel season starts again in the new year. The boat is laid up for a few months in the spring between the mackerel season coming to an end in March or April and the herring starting in June. Over those months holidays are taken, the gear is carefully overhauled ashore, and any work needed on the boat is completed.

A day out from Måløy, *Courage* was searching again for marks of mackerel close to the line between Norwegian and UK waters. That afternoon, George was in the wheelhouse with his attention on the sonars, scanning a strip of the sea a thousand metres wide, more than a little reminiscent of trying to find a needle in a haystack. With *Prowess* steaming to Norway with a catch of mackerel as *Courage* searched, George calculated that only 90 tonnes were left of the quota for the year.

Towards afternoon some scattered marks could be seen on the sonar, red patches fringed with green edged tendrils showing between the heavy side lobes of the echoes on both sonars. George brought *Courage* round in easy circles with touches of the autopilot to take a closer look at one of the more promising marks and to have a quick look with the echo sounder.

"Now we'll see what they are," he said as the mark began to inch across the sounder screen. "They're mackerel all right," he concluded a few moments later. "I wasn't sure if it was mackerel at first, but it shows on the high frequency. It's often difficult to tell at this time of the year. Could be forty, fifty tonnes."

Switching to manual steering, George kept circling the shoal at slow speed, gently adjusting the throttle and pitch of the propeller, watching the shoal to get an idea of its density, and to work out where it was heading and how fast.

"They seem to be going south-west. So we'll go south-west as well."

He explained that mackerel marks can be deceptive. If the shoal is seen head on to the sonar, it can give a much smaller mark and appear smaller than it would if the fish are swimming broadside to the sonar scan.

Once he was happy that he had a good idea of how it was behaving, he flicked all of the switches on the intercom system and murmured into the mouthpiece.

"Away the dahn, boys, away the dahn."

Below in the accommodation, the crew jumped up from their seats in the galley and in the TV room, and struggled into boots and oilskins, pulling on gloves and helmets before making their way out onto the deck to get ready to shoot.

99

At the stern, deckhand Ali Maitland waited with the drogue that replaced the dahn buoy used years ago in purse seining. Instead of a dahn buoy dropped with the end of the net, as was done in the past, the purse wire from the purse winch under the whaleback leads aft to the net bin and goes way when the net is shot. But the old terminology remains in use.

As George sounded a series of short blasts on the whistle, Ali heaved the drogue over the side. As it hit the water, the drogue caught the water and began to pull the net out from the net bin, slowly at first, then with gathering speed until the netting rushed over the rail quicker than the eye could follow. Moments later the weights of the leadline were running over the rail with a deafening clatter into the water.

With half of the seine away, the mark on the sonar was less clear.

"I think they're diving a bit," Alistair the mate said, with his eyes on the sonar screen.

"It's sinking reasonably quick," George replied, after switching on the Scanmar set, which relays the depth of the seine from the sensor attached to the middle of the seine's leadline.

"All gone," was heard from below as the last of the purse rings shot off the rail and into the water and the wedge wire started to pay out.

"Haul up your fore end at full speed," George called into the intercom, and a second later called out of the window.

"Stop paying out your after wire" to James and Stanley at the wedge wire winch directly under the wheelhouse.

The wheelhouse shuddered alarmingly as George used both bow and stern thrusters at full power, keeping the boat away from the seine and using the noise and turbulence to discourage the fish from making their way out of the circle of the net through the open area under the boat itself. The wedge wire winch started up again, and soon the leader rope was run through the triplex to start bringing the seine on board. Joe and Richard in the net bin hauled on the rope as the triplex fought to grip and take it through the rollers.

"Purse away full speed," George called into the intercom. "Aye, there's fish there all right," he said, indicating the mark still showing on the sonar inside the encircling ring of the seine.

"I thought we'd scooped some of it. It went very quick up to the net. We've got some, but I don't know if it's going to be enough to reach our target. In daylight at this time of year mackerel stay away from the net. You won't see much until the net's all alongside."

"Yes, yes, they're there," he said, pointing to a definite bulge in the line of the net showing on the sonar screen at the point furthest away from the side.

The ring almost closed, with most of the 20 tonne purse seine now back in the net bin.

With most of the purse seine in the bin behind him, James reaches for one of the last of the purse rings.

An hour's hard labour later, with the seine stacked back in the bin and the bag of the net alongside, the crew manhandled the heavy rubber hose into place and the crane dropped the pump over the side and into the water, suspended just below the surface. Water sprayed in every direction from the joins between hoses as the pumps started and the mackerel and water were sucked up from the net and through the separator on the hatch cover. A few moments later the first fish began to drop through the chute and down into the refrigerated sea water below, already chilled to a degree below freezing to keep the fish in top condition for the long steam to shore.

"You ought to see it when we're fishing for herring," Joe said to me as we watched the pump suck the glistening jewelled fish from the net. "There's a lot more to see. There's not a lot to see with mackerel because they stay at the bottom of the net, but the herring come to the top and it's like watching a boiling cauldron of fish sometimes with a good shot of herring."

This haul was estimated to be around 80 tonnes, stored in the forward RSW tanks in the same amount of chilled water. As evening came on, and with a few tonnes left of the quota, George prepared to shoot away again on another mark.

This time the shot was not a success, and two hours' hard work in the dark and the wet resulted in only a few fish, which were released back into the ocean. George put the boat's catch onto the evening auction.

"That should be it for 1999," George said as he set a course for Norway again, but before having received any confirmation of a buyer in Norway.

"We'll most probably be going back to Fraserburgh after this, so will you be coming with us or do you want to get a flight home?

"I'll stay with you if that's all right. My car's in Fraserburgh anyway."

"That's perfectly all right with us."

The West family (one of several fishing families in Fraserburgh with the same name) has been involved in fishing for several generations. "My mother's father had a boat called the *Livelihood*, and my father's father had a boat as well, the *Golden West*," George explained.

Then it looked as if fishing would skip a generation as George West senior left school and became a carpenter, working in shipyards locally, and later on the Clyde.

"My mother's brother had an accident at sea, so my grandfather asked my father to run the boat, so his first charge at sea was the

103

Livelihood. Then one year we were on holiday when we got a phone call to tell us that the *Livelihood* had been rammed and sunk, with no loss of life. We were without a boat for a few years before it was decided to build a boat with the intention of drifting and seine netting."

At that time herring was a huge industry, based on drift netting, while purse seining was something very new and unknown in Scotland, although it had been in done in Norway for many years.

"My father was asked if he would be interested in giving this new way of fishing a go, as the Norwegians had been making a success of it, and the result was that the *Prowess* was built as a purser."

The method was different then, with a second smaller boat used to help shoot the seine, and the fishing gear was also much smaller and lighter at that time, but hauled using a powerblock, a relatively recent invention at that time.

"We were fishing for herring all the year round in the Minches and off Shetland. In summer we would go as far as the deep water on the west side of Shetland. It was a great success, it worked well and we were content with that."

"As I got into my teens I got fed up with school. I was attracted to fishing and knew that I could go straight into a decent berth. I'd been away and enjoyed it, so I wasn't hard to persuade," George said.

George's elder brother David had already gone to sea in the *Prowess* with their father, and although he had done well at school and his parents had encouraged him to stay on in education, he decided to leave and follow the family into fishing.

"My father said that if they're both going to go to sea, we had better get another boat. So plans were drawn up for a new boat at Hall Russell's yard in Aberdeen."

George West left school in 1974, and the same year the *Courage*, a 90', 750 horsepower steel hulled purse seiner, was launched. Over the years, *Courage* served the family well, and was eventually sold to a Norwegian company in 1996, by which time it had grown into a 37 metre vessel with a 1600 horsepower engine. The same year the present *Courage* was bought from the Shetlands as a replacement. The original *Prowess* was also sold to become a whitefish trawler, and eventually replaced with a 52 metre Canadian boat originally built in Norway to work alternately as a seiner and as a sealer.

"Fishing has changed," George West continued. "The herring collapsed in the 1970s and there was a four year closure on the west coast and a six year closure in the North Sea. What then happened was that we realised we could catch mackerel, so it wasn't a disaster, it was a blessing in disguise."

"There had been some mackerel fishing, but no huge quantity. But mackerel was cheap, and we were looking at catching more, so the boats grew and the nets became stronger, with everything geared for fishing in quantity. This was nearly all off the west coast, with a small North Sea fishery in the middle of summer."

The next step was when the Scottish fleet discovered in the late 1970s that mackerel could also be fished successfully in the south west, to the extent that pursers from Scotland were spending half of every year, from October to the following March or April, in waters off Cornwall. Much of the fish landed went to Klondykers, factory vessels from African or Communist bloc nations that would anchor in Cornish or Scottish waters to take fish from local vessels for freezing or canning on board.

"The herring opened up again in '83," George said. "But the prices were nothing fancy. The fishery had been opened for everybody and there was herring available throughout Europe. Before the closure there had been a shortage of herring and prices were good. During the closure stocks recovered but the markets collapsed, the factories closed and people seemed to have lost the taste for herring. We were getting more for herring when it opened, £135 a tonne, than we are now. We were getting £100 a tonne this year, and there's no sign of it getting any better."

The appearance of the Atlanto-Scandian herring, with quotas totalling 1.4 million tonnes annually for the past few years, has not improved the prices, as this has flooded markets even further.

The Atlanto-Scandian herring is a huge fishery, and one that collapsed in the 1960s in waters around Iceland and the Faroes under the weight of massive over fishing. The recovery of this stock over the intervening 25 years is one of the wonders of the pelagic fishery, and took many fishermen by surprise.

"We knew the fish was there," George said. "We had been getting big spring spawning herring (unlike the summer spawning North Sea herring) north east of the Butt of Lewis and north west of Shetland, but we didn't realise that it was part of a bigger stock. It was only later that we realised what we'd been catching."

The Atlanto Scandian herring was also the first fish that *Courage* caught after the West family bought the boat from Shetland, steaming for days straight to fishing grounds around Jan Mayen from the slipway in Shetland.

"They are not so good to eat," George commented. "And more of it should go for fishmeal to keep the North Sea industry and markets healthy."

Ship's cook Ian Whyte at work on one of a great many fine meals.

Searching for fish. George West adjusts the settings on one of the array of sonars in *Courage*'s wheelhouse.

The mackerel fishery has also changed over the years, and fish that the Scottish fleet used to fish for in western waters has gradually shifted, to the extent that licences to fish for mackerel in the autumn months now have derogations to allow this fishery on the doorstep of the Norwegian area.

"The mackerel used to start off the north coast of Scotland, and they would migrate through the Minches to Ireland. Then one year they went along the west side of the Hebrides and since then they have travelled further and further north and east all the time."

"We never expected to be fishing for mackerel on the edge of the Norwegian sector," he said. "The scientists backed us up, so we are fishing here for west of Scotland mackerel. I'm not saying there's any super abundance of fish out there," he added, "but there's enough for everyone to make a living."

This highlights one of the biggest problems with the regulations that now hems in every fisherman. Legislation is generally a year or two, and often more than that, behind the fishery itself.

"All our problems are political ones," he commented at one point.

"The fishing patterns move much faster than legislation can catch up," George said. "It's constantly behind the times. You can see a change happening, and then it takes two years for a trend to be identified. Then we can go to our people and tell them what's happening and ask for what we need. Then they can take it to Europe..." George shrugged his shoulders and left the subject there.

The politics of the fishing industry are enormously complex, and in general George prefers to avoid discussing politics, but admits freely that his family has done well out of fishing. This has been built up into a business worth several million pounds as the demand for fishing licences has caused the prices of licences and quotas to spiral upwards.

Pelagic fishing is no longer a business that newcomers can enter without having much more financial backing than most fishermen would have at their disposal. He added that any licences that are for sale are normally snapped up immediately by the Dutch pelagic trawler companies that operate as international fisheries groups with vessels under a variety of flags.

"I used to hold the opinion and argue at meetings that the quotas belonged to those who had established them. Now my belief is that the quota really belongs to the whole community, everyone who has had a hand in it, the crew, the netmakers ashore, engineering firms, down to the local grocer."

But the fact remains that the quotas are extremely valuable and internationally sought after commodities that remain in the effective hands of fishing vessel operators.

"Of course, we could sell everything," George said one day while we were searching for mackerel. "But then what would my son do?"

Alexander West, due to leave school shortly, will join *Courage* as a 'deckie learner' on a fraction of a full deckhand's share, and a full berth will only be available to him when one becomes free.

"Most of the crew stay for years. Stanley's been the longest, he's been here for fifteen years. Joe and Johnny came on board at the end of last year. Our chief engineer left to join a bigger boat, and Martin didn't have his chief's ticket at the time - he's got it now - so we advertised for a chief and Johnny was the choice."

Berths for deck crew do not come up frequently, and Alexander West could have to wait some time for a full deckhand's job. The route from learner to deckhand is one that includes much that has to be learned.

"I expect a deckhand to be able to mend and splice, and to understand how the fishing gear works. They should be able to work on their own initiative to an extent, and to be able to see all the jobs that need doing on a boat, and eventually to keep a watch," George explained. "Some can do it in a matter of months, and others take longer over it."

"Ålesund this time," one of the crew coming off steaming watch announced coming into the messroom. "We're going to see the skipper's friend again."

The following morning *Courage* was again steaming into a Norwegian fjord to land, this time to a processor in one of the larger towns. It was a grey day with the occasional squall of rain as George brought *Courage* around the point and into sight of Ålesund itself, a pretty town built right down to the waters' edge, a mass of brightly painted roofs against a tree lined backdrop, picked out by the patchy bright sunshine.

We'll tie up in the town for an hour first," George said. "We're not due at the factory until one o'clock so you can go for a walk around Ålesund."

Courage eased gently up to the quay and the deckhands jumped ashore to tie up, mooring the boat to bollards on the quay a few feet from lorries and cars going along the busy main road leading out of the town.

"Everyone back on board at one o'clock British time," George murmured into the intercom, so that the echoing sound of his voice could be heard everywhere on board.

Almost everyone went ashore for a walk and a quick look at Ålesund, strolling through the rain among the wooden houses and picturesque quaysides, and taking a look at some of the plush shopping precincts as the rain beat down harder outside. Some of the boys returned to the boat with bags of fresh shrimp bought from inshore fishermen on the dock, and George came back with a cigar the size of a telegraph pole.

"I allow myself one if the fishing's going particularly well," he said, lighting up in the boat's TV room, the only place on board where smoking is allowed.

With all the crew back on board, the ropes were thrown off and Courage steamed slowly the short distance to the other side of the fjord and the West Fish factory to discharge. It was such a short distance that the crew did not even bother to go inside, standing on the whaleback, laughing and joking and admiring the rugged Norwegian scenery.

This processing plant was different to the one in Måløy in that it is located below a fertile pine clad hillside, in the middle of an industrial area, a few yards from where a small coaster was being noisily loaded with scrap metal. The crashes as each grab load of steel dropped into the hold punctuated the rest of the day as Courage's mackerel was pumped ashore.

Again a Japanese inspector stood by the conveyor belt that carried the fish into the bowels of the West Fish factory, carefully filleting samples of fish to check for quality, fat content and the type of feed to be found in the stomachs of the fish.

"Good fish," he said cryptically, pointing to a handful of dismembered fish on top of the conveyor belt's cover. "But this red feed is not good."

A day out from Ålesund, Courage was steaming towards Fraserburgh, when the plan of action changed. George was now searching for mackerel marks not far from where the first shots had been taken at the start of the trip.

"How anxious are you to get home?" George asked me half way across the North Sea.

"I'm not too worried. But it would be helpful to be ashore before the weekend."

"That's all right then. We'll have you ashore by Thursday at least. We might have to put you ashore in Shetland if we go there to get one of the radios repaired. But you can catch the ferry to Aberdeen easily enough. I'll find out for you when it goes."

"How much quota do you have left?"

"Well, none," George replied with a grin. "But we have a chance of trading some fish."

"Trade mackerel for something else?"

"Yes. Cash," George said with a wider grin. "There's a possibility of doing a deal to catch some of another boat's quota in exchange for a share

Hauling the purse seine. Mate Alistair Gibson at the netstacker's controls.

Richard Strachan clamping sections of the hose together to pump the fish aboard.

A serious looking Joe Cardno leans over the rail to check the fish being pumped from the bag of the net.

The mackerel start to jump and look for a way out as the net closes around them.

of the price. At £360 a tonne, we can still do some good business if we get a good shot. It went wrong for us last year," he admitted. "We traded for some quota and ended up with a fishmeal landing."

George looked at his watch. "I'll try him again. Kickoff isn't yet, so he'll probably talk to me."

A half shouted conversation followed over the satellite phone in the chartroom at the back of the wheelhouse. George came back smiling.

"Ninety tonnes," he announced. This extra quota had been bought from another Fraserburgh boat in a deal concluded in a few minutes before the start of a football match in the TV that the other vessel's owner was anxious not to miss.

The crew were less impressed with the change of plan, and over tea and smokes they complained quietly amongst themselves. "They do all right out of it, but for us it's less money. It isn't worth it for us catching this fish once the expenses have all come off the top."

In the wheelhouse, George was searching for marks, with his attention firmly on the sonar screen again. He pointed to the plotter screen, and showed the boat's tracks of a few days before at the top of the display, and the circular course that he had followed watching a shoal before shooting around it. The little green ship icon was visible on the same screen, half a dozen miles from where we had been to start with.

The radar screen showed dozens of echoes, mostly oil and gas rigs dotted over the North Sea. Looking out of the wheelhouse window, rigs could be seen on the horizon in every direction, practically every one with a bright orange plume of flame showing excess gas being burned off and a long black wedge of smoke leading skywards. Each rig has a small puppy dog of a support ship at is ankles, ready to shoo away fishing boats that stray too close to the platforms.

A scattering of small marks showed on the sonar, and George looked at each one carefully, taking *Courage* round in a wide arc each time, and going closer for a look with the dual frequency echo sounder at anything that looked promising. "Small fish give harder marks. If a mark shows well on the high frequency and reasonably well on low frequency, you can be fairly sure that it's small mackerel."

Pointing at a mark on the sonar screen he explained that when fishing for herring the marks are much more solid. "Herring normally give much harder marks, with none of these hairy bits," he said, meaning the lighter green fringes round the red centres of the marks.

The aroma of frying steaks from the galley filled the whole ship as cook Ian Whyte prepared the evening meal. Steak and chips with mounds of salad for Saturday.

George's attention was constantly on the sonars as he tweaked the tilt and train controls to monitor a shoal that looked to be a likely proposition. Taking a second look at a mark that did not seem to be a big one, George circled it for a second time.

"We'll buzz them and see what happens," he said, half to himself. A minute later the echo sounder showed clearly the mark on the high frequency side of the display, with a less distinct mark running parallel to it on the low frequency side.

Every few minutes he twisted the autopilot to bring the boat around further to starboard, before eventually switching over to manual steering.

"Away the dahn, boys, away the dahn," he murmured into the intercom.

"That's going to make them happy, with dinner nearly ready," Alistair chuckled from the corner by the window.

"Aye, they'll be moaning now," George answered with a smile.

Down in the galley Ian put the steaks into a tray ready to be reheated after the shot. A huge tray of green salad and tomatoes was carefully covered with clingfilm and put to one side, and the uncooked chips stayed in their plastic bucket, ready to be fried later.

The dahn dropped over the side into the wake as darkness began to fall. George brought *Courage* round in a neat circle as the shouts from the deck told him how many rings had gone off the bar. As the circle closed, George used the bow and stern thrusters to discourage the fish from swimming out under the boat. As both thrusters pumped water at full speed, everything shook and rattled, and the floor of the wheelhouse vibrated under our feet.

As the wedge wire was quickly brought in and the leader to the net run through the triplex, the sonar screen showed a neat circle of the net, with the mark clear in the centre.

"Smack in the middle," Alistair said appreciatively.

"I'll get the hang of this one day," George replied with a wider than usual smile on his face.

"A nice circle is better for that shot," he explained. "Better than shooting a banana shape and having to pull the ends in. But they're cunning devils and sometimes we shoot in a long shape like a banana and then wait for the fish to build up in the net."

Despite the crew's original misgivings, there were grins all round as Richie handed round the customary coffee from the tray brought from the galley while the fish were pumped aboard. The shot looked to be a good one, guessed to be around 70 tonnes. The mackerel also began to show themselves earlier this time, a few at the top fighting in vain to get out of the net, and some walking on their tails across the pool.

This was the last of the mackerel for the trip. A second shot later that evening was a washout, and George put the catch onto the auction later that evening, worried that fish auctioned late on a Saturday evening would not be attractive for a processor to work on a Sunday when staff would expect to be paid at a higher rate.

After the final shot, George decided to sit tight for a few hours outside the Norwegian zone to wait for a reply. Despite having a fully legal catch taken in UK waters, he preferred not to have to deal with any questions from the notoriously thorough Norwegian fisheries protection service, who could be suspicious about a British purser hove to in their waters with fish on board.

This time *Courage*'s destination was Sirevåg, a small fishing village a little way north of Egersund, where the *Prowess* was also due to discharge its catch.

Steaming through the oilfields again, rigs and standby boats were everywhere. In the half light of early morning, every rig had its plume of orange flame, and one particularly large rig burned a flame of such intensity that its light illuminated ravines and planes in the low hanging grey clouds, tinting the thick cloudbase all around with an unhealthy orange glow.

The weather was freshening for a gale forecast for the next day. Approaching Sirevåg in the dark that night, George watched the two radar screens carefully. The entrance was a narrow one, and this was the first time that he had been here. Between glancing from radar to plotter and back again to check his position, he said that he preferred to enter the unfamiliar port in the dark than to wait for daylight and go in with the south westerly gale that had been forecast for the following morning.

Alistair the mate stood at the window in the corner of the wheelhouse with his hand on the control lever of the big searchlight, painstakingly picking out the few buoys that marked the channel.

Checking again against the chart, George brought *Courage* over a few degrees as he picked up the two red leading lights that mark the course to steer to the harbour mouth. Closer to the shore now, Alistair on the searchlight picked out the grey rocks that lined the shoreline, and the narrow harbour entrance. As this was little more than half as wide again as *Courage*, George used both bow and stern thrusters to keep clear of the sloping shelves of stone on one side and the breakwater on the other, and relaxed visibly as *Courage* glided into the calm waters of the small harbour.

Prowess was already in, tied up further along the quay, and several of *Prowess*' crew immediately made their way along to take our ropes and come on board for coffee and a yarn in the galley.

Early in the morning landing started, and the sparkling mackerel, fresh from being kept at close to freezing point, were pumped onto the factory's conveyor and into the building. The now familiar figure of the Japanese quality control inspector could be seen picking out fish at random to fillet and examine their innards.

"George isn't happy," one of the crew said in the messroom over breakfast. "He was told it was seventy tonnes, but he booked in ninety, and it looks like it's going to be seventy."

"Has he bought any more quota?" another voice asked through a mouthful of porridge.

"Don't know. He was talking about horse mackerel earlier."

"Oh, aye."

"Well, we'll just have to wait and see. Should be back to the Broch tomorrow and get ready for the sprats."

"Unless he buys some more mackerel."

"We'll find out soon enough."

"That's right lads. It's not over until the ropes are on at the Broch," the first voice summed up.

Discussion and speculation continued throughout the morning as the fish were pumped ashore, and that afternoon *Courage* sailed from Sirevåg into some uncomfortably rough weather, with a course set for Fraserburgh. By now it was clear that the mackerel fishing was over, and the crew would all be home the following evening. Everyone relaxed, George left the wheelhouse to the mate and the crew to take steaming watches back across the North Sea, and the videos came out again. With all of the rented stock having been watched over and again, tapes appeared from cabins with even more war and gangster epics to while away the long steam.

Courage punched through the waves throughout the night and all through the following day. Steaming watches changed every few hours and tapes were replaced in the video player, while meals came and went on the long messroom tables. Cards and chessmen came out, and many of the crew retired to cabins to read, sleep, or listen to the CD players that almost every cabin had, each one tied to the table to prevent it rolling off in the worst of the weather. In the afternoon, Grampian TV could be received on board, and not long afterwards the coast of Scotland appeared in sight.

"You know you're almost home when you get Grampian TV again," Tigger announced as he fiddled with the tuning of the television set to improve the fuzzy reception.

With a few hours left to go, the crew disappeared one by one and reappeared showered and shaved, ready to go ashore.

It was past nightfall when George brought *Courage* into Fraserburgh harbour, gently conning the boat through the gaps only just wide enough to squeeze through with touches of the bow and stern thrusters. *Courage* was eased into place and tied up outside *Prowess*, which had left Sirevåg early in the morning and had been a few hours ahead of us all the way across the North Sea.

Fraserburgh was asleep as I shook hands all round and said my farewells to George and the crew. There were already a few cars with engines idling on the quay, with wives waiting to take their husbands home. The crew dispersed quickly, each one anxious to get home after eleven days away from home, but Tigger, Richie and Ali still had time to hand my bags ashore for me, passing them over the yawning gap between *Courage* and *Prowess* and then up onto the quay.

While I had been at sea, a thick layer of salty grime had accumulated on the windows of my car, parked outside the Fishermen's Mission, in which someone had fingered 'wash me' in wobbly letters. By the time I had walked the hundred yards around the dock and fetched the car, most of the crew had already departed, leaving on board only George and engineers Johnny and Martin, who had stayed on board to take fuel, preferring to do it straight away than come back in the morning. With the main engine shut down, *Courage* lay dormant at the quayside, until the start of the sprat season in a week or two.

The art of purse seining - fishing in perfect weather.

117

Skipper David Stevens watches from the wheelhouse window as the gear is shot away for the first haul of the trip.

5

November - *Crystal Sea*, Newlyn

Trawling In The Wild West

This is practically as far west as it is possible to go in mainland Britain, and Cornwall hardly feels like a part of part of the same country. It is a corner of Britain that is alternately fertile and barren, with rich farmland and fishing grounds, often separated by harsh rocks and bleak moors.

In addition, I have a personal soft spot for Newlyn more than anywhere else in Britain, and it's one of the few places that tries to call me back to it.

It was already dark by the time I found the *Crystal Sea* moored by the ice plant in Newlyn. Skipper David Stevens, a broad, weatherbeaten man with an equally broad smile and a shock of black hair shot with grey, was stood at the hatch in the shelterdeck as the two crewmen manhandled boxes into place two levels below in the boat's fishroom. As each pair of boxes was dropped into place directly under the hatch, David lowered the landing gear down to the bowels of the boat where the two iron hooks were snapped onto the bottom box and the pair were hauled up and into the open air. Here the agent's men on the truck at the quayside hauled on a rope to bring the boxes sailing over to the platform. Moments later the empty hooks and chains were swinging back and down into the fishroom again as the truck's crew struggled with the weight of the boxes.

This was a half landing, David explained between lifts. The *Crystal Sea* had sailed from Newlyn before the weekend, and taking the advice of Robin the agent, David had decided that the following day's market looked likely to be one of the better ones of the week.

I had been trying to arrange a trip with him for several months, but the weather had intervened several times, and then the eclipse and other events posed a few difficulties, and it was not until late in the year that I was on my way back to Cornwall. We had spoken the day before over a crackling cellphone connection, while David was in the wheelhouse watching the warps creep across the top of the shelterdeck.

"If you want to come with us we'll be in tomorrow night for a few hours. We'll want to be away about nine, so is that all right for you?"

Twenty-four hours later I was standing on the *Crystal Sea*'s shelterdeck talking to him at last and waiting to sail.

"We're just throwing a few boxes ashore now. We'll want to be away in about an hour, once we've taken some ice. I've just got some of this paperwork to sort out, and then we'll be off."

Once the sixty odd boxes were safely in the truck and landed, *Crystal Sea*'s crewmen Mark 'Tuc' Laity and David's son 'Boy' David Stevens made their way up to the deck and from there on to the quay.

Tuc, a rawboned former Coldstream guardsman, was the newest member of the crew, and only on his second trip with the boat. Apart from a spell ashore recovering from an injury at sea, Boy David has worked with his father since leaving school. The fourth crew member, David's younger son Alec, was away sitting his ticket in Fraserburgh.

Tuc and Boy David departed to help the agent and his helper to put the fish in the chiller ready for the morning's market, leaving David senior to hose down the fishroom and get ready for the ice. When the crew reappeared, a hose from the ice plant was dropped through the hatch and down to the fishroom. Tuc pulled on a pair of ear defenders and made his way down below, where he angled the flexible end of the hose, made up of a series of metal rings, into one of the forward pounds. The reason for the ear defenders was soon clear as the ice began to flow with a deafening rattle through the hose to pile up behind the wooden pound boards. The *Crystal Sea* does not sail without four or five tonnes of ice in the fishroom's forward compartment. The hose has a life of its own with the ice rattling through it from the plant high above the quay, and Tuc battled to keep it steady and the ice streaming into the right pound.

Hatches closed and dogged down, boxes of bait dropped on the deck of one of the local crabbers, and the *Crystal Sea* cruised gently past rows of beamers and netters at the quay out of the harbour into the swell from the easterly wind. Steaming southwards, the lights of Newlyn dimmed gradually behind, the lights of Mousehole winked off our starboard side, and the *Crystal Sea* bucked gently in the fresh wind.

"She's a tiger this one, she'll roll a bit now, but when it freshens a bit she'll be as steady as you like," Tuc said. "It's a good berth this one. Made up with it," he added.

"There's not been a lot of fish about," David observed. "We came in closer today and did a bit better, so that's where we'll be going again now."

"And we'll be keeping quiet about it," Boy David added.

David also explained some of the boat's rules. "When you turn in, or if you go aft for a piss, you tell the man on watch so he always knows where everyone is." Another rule, unusual on most fishing boats, is that everyone wears a lifejacket on deck, and mine was handed to me shortly before we shot away. These are self inflating jackets that strap on like a waistcoat, and contrary to popular opinion, they don't get in the way.

"There's nothing wrong with them," Tuc said. " This is the first time I've been on a boat where I've been told 'you will wear a lifejacket.' But you forget you've got it on. You go forward and start gutting and realise that you're still wearing the thing."

Clear of the harbour, the deck lights were switched on at the stern, and Boy David set to work on the codend of the trawl with a knife and a handful of needles loaded with twine. He systematically went over the single braided twine of the codend, replacing parted meshes when needed, and adding the long strands of bright orange rope, known as dollies, that protect the netting from abrasion on the seabed.

David took his ticket five years ago, and skippers the boat when his father takes a trip off. "I never really thought of doing anything else," he said, sitting on the net in the pound and plying a needleful of twine as I carefully split dollies into two. "I did well at school, but didn't really want to stay."

"There is a stigma attached to fishermen," he explained as the *Crystal Sea* chugged out into the gentle swell. "People think they're stupid and drink a lot. Maybe it's because the ones they see are ones who act stupid ashore, but it is annoying. They don't see the hard working ones, because they're always at sea."

Crystal Sea is one of the hardest working boats in Newlyn, and reckoned to be one of the port's top berths, but stop-overs between trips when the weather is good enough for fishing are short, just long enough to land, refuel, take ice and stores, and if the crew are lucky, to grab a shower. Time off comes in the winter months when the weather worsens and can keep them in port for days or even weeks at a time.

"I hate it when we get a bad autumn," David said. "It makes the winter seem so long. Last year it started to blow in August, and we only got in half of August, September and October, and it went on right through to February like that. And this year looks like it's going to be the same."

A couple of hours and a dozen miles from Newlyn, Tuc and the two Davids pulled on oilskins and gloves ready to shoot the trawl away. Tuc and Boy David rolled the newly patched codend over the rail and let the belly stream astern in the velvet darkness. This was the light trawl, kept

Boy David at the winch, with a hand on each of the brakes as the bridles run off the drums.

Shooting away in the dark for a night time haul. David throwing one of the towing chains over the starboard warp.

David watching as the gear is hauled and the warps creep across the deck, passing instructions to Boy David at the winch under the shelterdeck.

' I'm a liner man, and liner men don't wear gloves'.
David unclipping the lazy deckie from the starboard door.

in a pound at the stern, while the hard ground trawl with its heavy duty rockhopper footrope is kept on the boat's single net drum.

The footrope rattled over the side, and the Boy David made his way forward to the winch, ready to slack out the bridles. With the trawl streamed fully astern, and responding to shouts from Tuc and David at the stern, he eased off the winch brakes and began to pay the gear away, with the 60 fathom sweeps, followed by 20 fathoms of split bridles running off the main barrels of the drums. As the splits reached their ends, the backstrops on the doors took the strain and the doors bucked gently with a life of their own.

In response to a shout from astern, Boy David eased back on the winch, leaving Tuc first to shackle up the pennant and then shackle the warp into the towing bracket on the port side, while David went through the same practised movements to starboard, all the while holding a conversation punctuated with shouts to the winch.

"We've got our heavy hopper gear on the drum, and for that the long bridles come off and we just shoot the splits. Woah! These are the best doors I've ever had. Clear starboard! Half tonne Morgeres, good as gold they are."

David made his way up to the wheelhouse and brought the boat around slightly before giving his instructions to Boy David at the winch under the shelterdeck through the squeaks and whistles of the intercom system.

"A hundred at the winch this time. One, zero, zero," as the winch drums began to roll with Boy David and Tuc at the brakes. The *Crystal Sea* bucked with freedom as the trawl dropped away astern, until the winch slowed and the boat began to take the strain of the gear.

David and Tuc each looped a chain stopper over a warp, and hooked one of the heavy duty rope and wire towing strops into it, calling to Boy David at the winch to slack away again and allow the strops to take the strain. Each warp was pulled off a few more feet to allow some slack, and the boat settled immediately into a steady motion with the trawl spread over the seabed 30 fathoms below.

"Now I've got the watch, unfortunately," David said as he poured water from the big kettle that is kept hot all the time into tea mugs on the table. As soon as the mugs had been emptied, Tuc, Boy David and I made our way below. The *Crystal Sea* is an old boat, built in Scotland at Macduff in 1974, and the layout is old fashioned, with a single cabin below decks for the crew's accommodation.

"You'd better have Alec's bunk over there," Tuc said down below, pointing to the far corner. With a few misgivings, I crawled into one of the cubbyhole bunks in the starboard side and rolled myself in my sleeping bag, tasted the musty air, and switched out the light to be left in total and impenetrable blackness. It seemed like only a few minutes later that the intercom was whistling and calling us out again to haul. In the galley three mugs of tea were waiting on the table, and these disappeared as layers of sweaters and damp oilskins were pulled on against the three o'clock in the morning chill.

Boy David went forward to the winch, and as the engine revs dropped away, he eased the warps in far enough for Tuc and David to take off the towing chains.

"Now we'll see if we're sucking the right titty," Tuc said as the warps rolled in. David was at the wheelhouse window with the intercom in his hand, and his eye on the starboard gallows, ready to pass on to Boy David forward that the doors were up.

As soon as the door eased its way up to the gallows, the winch came to a gentle halt and David was on the deck seconds later. The door was unshackled with swift movements, and with a shout of 'clear starboard', followed moments later by 'clear port' from Tuc on the far side, the bridles started to wind in through the blocks. A rattle announced the twin split bridles coming aboard, until moments later the wing ends appeared at the blocks and the winch came to a quick halt.

David freed the lazy deckie from the wing end and clipped it into a rope running outside the shelterdeck and forward to the hatch in the *Crystal Sea*'s starboard side. Boy David at the winch had braked up the main drums and unclutched them to allow the warping drum to turn, and he carefully dropped a couple of turns around it and began to wind in the codend, with the long rope leading away into the darkness. Tuc stood with a gilson at the ready, and as soon as the lifting becket appeared in the hatch, he dropped the short strop spliced into it over a spike to hold it, and hooked the double purchased gilson into the lifting becket. The poorly greased pulley above the hook began to squeal alarmingly as Boy David transferred the gilson rope to the drum and hauled it in, bringing the codend into the hatch to swing inside. Tuc quickly grabbed the codlines and as the codend swung wildly, he wrapped the rope leading to the clip deftly around a stanchion to keep it still and tapped the codend clip with a hammer to release it.

A flood of fish landed on the deck, and Tuc and David pulled stray fish from the meshes of the net. David made a rapid assessment of what the catch was before the codend was pulled tight and the clip hammered home again. Tuc shoved the codend back out through the hatch and into the water as David, back in the wheelhouse, brought the boat around to shoot away again. Boy David let the lazy deckie run out through his fingers until it was passed back aft and clipped onto the wing end.

In the meantime, Tuc pulled a couple of baskets from the stack and began sorting fish into them, soles, dories, brill and turbot into one basket, plaice, lemon soles and megrims in another, whiting, squid and cuttles each have a basket to themselves, crabs put to one side, monk thrown in the aluminium hopper at the side of the shelterdeck, and rays thrown into a separate basket by themselves. Pouts and spotty dogs, kept for pot bait, filled another couple of the big seven stone baskets.

The trawl was shot back into the darkness. With daylight not far off the stars glittered in the blackness, a narrow sliver of new moon rose past a bank of low cloud above the deep blue of the sky just before dawn, and the light of the Wolf Rock flashed regularly a dozen miles to the west.

With the fish picked up into baskets, Tuc and Boy David sharpened knives to start gutting. Boy David started on the flats, flipping them into another basket one by one, while Tuc headed the monkfish and gutted the basket of skate. David came down from the wheelhouse and started on the basket and half of whiting, gutting barehanded and dropping the fish one by one into another basket on the deck.

"I'm a liner man, and liner men don't wear gloves. Here, you're a beamer man," he said, passing a knife across to me. "You can give us a hand with these soles."

Fish are washed by hand on board the *Crystal Sea*, with one man holding a hose and the other carefully sluicing every speck of sand from the gills and each tinge of blood from the gut cavity. David claims never to have found a washer that does the job well enough, and swears by washing every fish individually.

"All done are we? Right, I'll leave you to it then," David said and disappeared back inside to get back to the wheelhouse. Meanwhile Tuc clambered down the iron ladder to the fishroom, and Boy David handed the baskets of gleaming clean fish down one by one to him, before climbing down as well and carefully shutting the hatch behind him.

The first tiers of boxes were laid out on the fishroom floor, each with a generous helping of crushed ice shovelled into it before the first fish was put to bed, with each fish lovingly put into place and carefully iced again as the boxes are filled. Newlyn's fishing boats do not catch large amounts of fish, so every fish is important, and quality is becoming an increasingly vital consideration.

"We carry around five tonnes of ice," David explained later. "That's for five or so days at sea. We used to carry a ton of ice for a week's lining

Emptying the codend, and a mass of fish drops onto the deck, monkfish, congers, plaice, megrims, lemon soles, dover soles, whitings, squid, cuttlefish, and hake, as well as the ever present starfish, plus a few crabs and lobsters.

Getting ready to shoot the trawl back as David unclips the gilson from the strop around the bag.

Tuc and Boy David at work in the fishroom. Each fish is put to bed individually, laid carefully into boxes with layers of ice.

With the trawl shot back, Tuc and Boy David pick up the fish, sorting them into baskets as they go.

The fatigue shows in David's face at the end of the trip, after a week at sea and never more than a few hours sleep at a time.

Top quality fish, hake, John Dory and dover sole, as fresh as they could possibly be.

Tuc shovelling some of the eight or so tonnes of crushed ice that the *Crystal Sea* carries in the fishroom. "You wouldn't think of going to sea with less than that," David said.

when I was starting fishing. You wouldn't even bother going now with that much ice on board."

Breath condenses in the clean chill air of the fishroom, and no more time is spent there than necessary. After breaking up some ice from the pound for use on the next haul, Tuc and David made their way back up to the deck and the mugs of tea once again ready for them on the galley table.

Fishing has changed in the years that David Stevens has been skipper, and some species have become scarce. The large gill netting fleet has all but disappeared, leaving only a handful of highly skilled fishermen to concentrate on it. The beam trawler fleet has also taken its toll on the south west grounds, and Newlyn's beamers are going through tough times.

"Out past the islands ten years ago, you'd get a basket of hake a go. Now you don't get a boxful for a trip. The netters have hammered it. Now they're going to these turbot nets, and they'll wonder why there's none left in a year or two."

"But you're starting to see a lot of small hake again," Boy David said as the morning haul was being gutted. "Now that the netters aren't chasing them so hard. But we haven't had what you'd call a hard winter now for a couple of years. The sea temperature is half a degree higher than last year, and that makes a difference."

"Should be cold winter this year," David commented, finishing the whitings and starting on the soles. "There's been that much fruit on the trees this year."

"And the leaves have been late falling as well," Boy David added. "It all points to a cold winter."

Incidentally, they were quite right and it was a cold wnter.

David picked up a solitary sole that had somehow slipped past the basket and was flapping its way towards the scupper. "If Big H was here he'd say that there's all the profit gone," he said with a grin as he gutted the fish and dropped it into the basket with the rest of the prime.

That afternoon in the wheelhouse David was working out his options, with the weather not looking at all favourable. "This easterly wind's no friend to anybody. It just cuts the fishing dead. They're giving out gales imminent now as well, so we might be going inside to see if we can make a day of it there."

Boy David and Tuc were in the galley watching a music video later that day in between hauls, munching apples and sandwiches over the usual mugs of tea when the call came to haul the gear. The tape was still running as they pulled on oilskins and sweaters.

"That's Shania Twain, isn't it?"

"Yup," Boy David replied, pulling on a third sweater and reaching for his oilskin trousers, wrapped around his boots.

"Nice, isn't she?"

"Didn't you know that's not her real name?"

"What's she called then?"

"Her real name's Eileen Edwards."

Tuc disappeared for a moment as he pulled on his oilskin top.

"Don't think I fancy her any more, then," he concluded and stopped the tape to go out on deck. "Not if she's an Eileen, doesn't seem the same somehow."

That afternoon's haul brought a similar amount of fish on board, and as darkness began to fall again, the weather had picked up to a fresh wind.

"You see how different she is now?" David asked. "When it's flat calm she's all over the place, but now there's some wind she just sits there." The boat's movement was certainly more regular and comfortable than it had been earlier in the day when the sea had been calmer, and the addition of a breeze also helped clear the fug inside, blasting draughts of fresh air in through the open shelterdeck door. "Mind you, she's got a mind of her own sometimes when you want to manoeuvre in the harbour. If she wants to go over there, you've just got to let her."

Tuc appeared in the wheelhouse, ready to take his watch for the tow, mug and baccy in hand.

"Now, I want you to do the same as you did last time," David told him with a smile before disappearing below for a few hours' sleep. "The state of the tide's almost the same and it's the same time of day, so I want you to see if you can find them again."

"I was surprised when David said he had trouble getting crew," Tuc said when David had gone below. "This is a good berth, I'm made up with it. David's a real gentleman, it's comfortable here. You know, there's space to sleep in and there's a toilet on board, none of that bucket and chuck it stuff. I've been netting mostly, and I was on a twin rigger for the summer. Two of us working twenty hours a day," Tuc said and shook his head at the memory of endless hours on deck and the impossibility of completing all of the jobs that need to be done on a fishing boat.

Incidentally, *Crystal Sea*'s toilet is a compartment between the accommodation and the engine room, with a bewildering series of valves that have to be opened and closed to ensure that the results of a visit actually go over the side.

The tow was a quiet one, and the seabed image on the colour sounder remained an unremitting steady line, punctuated with small marks not hard enough to be anything solid.

"We'll see what happens in a day or two if we go up past Longships on the hard ground with the hopper gear. That's real injun country and you'll see some proper bows and arrows there."

After a disappointing evening haul of a basket and a half of megrim, half a basket of prime and a couple of baskets of pot bait fish, Tuc dished up a magnificent bucket of spag bol, all stewed to perfection in a single pot on top of the oil fired cooker.

"It's not going to be a pile of fish, not with this easterly wind, but if we can keep going, all to the good," David said between mouthfuls of meat and pasta. Other boats had already made their way home to land for the next day's market, leaving the following day's market possibly short of fish.

That night Boy David took the tow, and at five in the morning the sound of the engine being throttled back brought everyone from their bunks without having to be called.

"Tight are we, Dave?" Tuc called up as he pulled on a sweater and oilskins.

"Yup. Almost calling out time anyway."

David was already in the wheelhouse and Boy David clattered down the steps to pull on his wet weather gear in the cramped galley and make his way forward to the winch. The warps rolled in gently, hauling cautiously, and by the time the doors were up and unshackled, the trawl was still caught on the seabed obstruction. Tuc stood at the stern waiting for the gear to come up, while David sat with his eyes glued on the wire coming through the starboard block. The sweeplines were visibly taught as they rolled gradually in and the boat's motion left no doubt that the trawl was still firmly fast on the bottom, when with a slight lurch of the boat, the wires began to run more quickly and the trawl was free.

"We'd better have a look at it," David called down, and with the wing ends in the blocks, he brought the *Crystal Sea* around in a wide arc to starboard to bring as much of the net out of the water as possible.

"There's something there in the tunnel," Tuc shouted, straining his eyes in the dark to see the net in the gloom at the edge of the circle of light around the boat. David came down to the deck and stood at the powerblock controls, bringing the heavy block on its hydraulic arm down to deck level. Tuc and Boy David struggled a bight of net over the block, and strained to start it pulling through. The netting caught, and the tunnel of the trawl was spun through until the obstruction could be reached. This turned out to be a yard long piece of aluminium, with every point of its jagged edges snagged on a mesh, thankfully without any damage to the trawl.

Fetching a gutting knife from inside the shelterdeck, David rapidly cut away a row of meshes in the fine netting, leaving a hole big enough to manhandle the surprisingly heavy metal out of the trawl. A few swift turns with a needle was enough to sew up the hole, and the codend was brought in as usual to leave half a dozen baskets of fish flapping on the deck. The trawl was shot back, and with the fish picked up into baskets, everyone took a knife and a basket and started gutting.

"Missed the forecast," David grumbled when the fish had all been washed and put away. Back in the galley teas were made and the TV switched on to wait for the next forecast.

"We'll wait and see what happens in the daylight," David added. "Mervyn sailed and turned back, says he's going to have a look again in the daylight."

At last the forecast appeared in the usual round of daytime television, and everyone's eyes followed the progress of the isobars over Cornwall as the week's expected weather unfolded.

"They're tightening up for Sunday," Boy David observed doubtfully.

"Looks a lot better after the weekend," Tuc added.

"Coming westerly as well," David commented. "Right, plan A is to be in for Saturday. The fish is mostly prime which can be sold locally so there's not a problem with exports. Sail Sunday night. It might still be poor weather, but we should be able to get a couple of days to the middle of the week at least. That's plan A, anyway."

That evening's meal was one of David's, a gammon roast of mammoth proportions.

"I hope you like roasties, coz I've done plenty," David said as the roasting tin was emptied onto the enamel plates that were already in danger of overflowing, followed by cauliflower and a small mountain of mashed swede and turnip.

"I've done all this veg because it was last trip's." David explained. "Now, where's the bisto gone?"

Everyone dug in manfully to make inroads into the vast plates of food, until David had to admit defeat.

"Anyone want any more?" he asked, pointing to his plate.

"Couldn't eat another thing, me."

"I'll have your meat, Dave," Tuc offered, and the remains of the gammon were scraped onto Tuc's plate. A few beads of sweat appeared on his forehead as he battled with the mountain of food.

"You're not going to manage it."

"I'll manage all right."

"No, you'll never get through that lot."

"I will. Just you wait and see."

A few minutes later knife and fork clattered onto a clean plate, and Tuc grinned with triumph. "I was struggling a bit at the end," he admitted, reaching for his baccy pouch.

On the television news that evening was an item about scientists calling for 50% cuts in cod and haddock quotas, the annual figure tossed out as a political starting point for the negotiations over the next year's quotas.

As the reporter intoned the usual platitudes about British fishermen catching less than a third of the cod they were catching twenty years ago and the prices of fish currently being higher than they have ever been, the crew added their own observations.

"Of course we are. Twenty years ago we had a deep sea fleet that was second to none fishing all over the Arctic. And fish prices haven't gone up at all for cod and haddock, only for luxury fish, the stuff that restaurants buy like turbot and monk, and then they haven't gone up anywhere near in line with inflation."

A few seconds of the usual stock footage of Peterhead fish market accompanied the item, followed by a very brief interview with the chief executive of one of the fishermen's organisations blaming the government for its weak stance in negotiating quotas with the rest of Europe.

With the news over and the television switched off, Tuc went up to the wheelhouse to take the next tow, and the two Davids turned in.

The next haul, very early in the morning, was another poor one, with a basket of prime and half a basket of flatfish. "Crab city in here," Tuc said as we picked up the fish from the deck, and collected a dozen big brown crabs from the corners they had retreated into, while spider crabs were pitched back over the side.

David brooded in the wheelhouse. "You've got to keep at it. If you weren't here, you'd just look at the forecast and you wouldn't go. Nice weather ashore. Couldn't ask for nicer weather. Paint the boat, do what you want. But here..." he shrugged and didn't bother to finish the sentence.

"There's no bloody fish here, and I know there's no bloody fish out there either. There's no point moaning about it. The wind's gone a bit more easterly," he observed. "Up in the Bristol Channel it doesn't seem to make a difference, but down here it cuts everything dead. We could go up the Channel, but there's no point going all that way for two or three hauls. We'd have to make a day or two of it, and then we'd be landing next week in the best of the weather. We're not going anywhere now," he said finally. "Two more hauls and that'll be tally."

David Stevens has fished all his life, starting with his father immediately after leaving school on the family boat from St Ives. The *Rose of Sharon* was a longliner, fishing in waters close to home with a large crew of seven men. But fishing in inshore waters was no easy game, and working from St Ives leaves fishing boats at the mercy of the tide.

"We used to catch our own bait. We had an 18' gig and a ring net, like a purse net but with the bunt in the middle, and seven men in this boat. Three forward, three aft and one in the middle with a big oar frightening the sandeels into the net. You'd go at three in the morning to catch your bait, and some days you'd have a job to catch it."

The sandeels were then put on board the *Rose of Sharon*, and the lines would be baited by hand into baskets while steaming to the fishing grounds. Once the line was shot, it would be left to soak for four or five hours, allowing some of the crew to snatch some sleep, before it was hauled, which was the best part of a day's work. Back in St Ives at the end of the day, the fish was landed onto a lorry to be taken to be sold in Newlyn, by which time there were only a few hours of the day left before the whole process began all over again at three the next morning.

"Lining was labour intensive. You wouldn't get the men together to do that now. People wouldn't do it now. If you had three hours sleep in twenty-four, that was about it. On Saturday you'd sleep all afternoon, then do your bit of courting or whatever it was you wanted to do, and on Sunday night you'd be turned in early to be up to catch your bait on Monday morning."

"We were lining in coves from St Ives to the Longships and on the Brisons and the White Spot. It was all blond rays and turbots, but that finished when cray netting came in, all the blond rays were caught before they came inshore. And now we can see the same thing happening again."

There were hard times as well, and the weather stopped fishing as frequently as it still does in the south west. "One winter we never cast off for eleven weeks," David remembered. "You'd go to the loft and make up your gear for the next season. But that particular winter we ran out of work to do, and father said, 'Right. We'll go home and paint the house.'"

That was the year that David and Margaret were courting, and he recalled that her family were less than impressed with him, thinking him workshy with the boat tied up for weeks on end, an impression that he was able to dispel later.

At that time a fisherman was capable of commanding good earnings, roughly double what a tradesman ashore would be able to expect. "You used to work that hard, and a tradesman earned twelve or sixteen quid a week," he said. "But that comparison isn't there any more. That could be

"East wind's no friend to anyone." Getting the trawl on board at the end of the trip.

Muffled aganst the stinging wind, Tuc and Boy David pack the trawl down into the pound at the stern of the boat.

the reason for youngsters not wanting to come into it any more. We're not making any more for our fish now than when we first bought this boat. The 80s were the best times for the prices of fish, and the costs of materials weren't so high. A set of warps was 500 quid then, and they're about two grand now."

In the 1970s pelagic trawling for mackerel and pilchards started in Cornwall, and with his father's illness and untimely death, the young David Stevens found himself commanding the *Rose of Sharon* when barely out of his teens, midwater fishing in the summer and lining through the winter.

"We had it off to a tee, with no headline gear or anything. I was 21 then, midwater fishing for mackerel as a pair team with Michael Hosking. His boat was the *Kilravock*, built in Macduff in 1947 or 48, and bought from Beaumaris. She was 65', the same as the *Rose of Sharon*."

Pelagic fishing was a welcome boost for fishermen in Cornwall, but turned out to be short lived, and now there is limited fishing in Cornish waters, and practically none for local boats, apart from a handful of handliners fishing for mackerel.

"We had two years on the pilchards and then the mackerel set in." David recalls. "Then the Scots started to come down here as well. That was fun and games, but the last good season for local boats was 1978-79."

The mackerel were no longer in such plentiful supply, and by that time David had also left the family boat to work for W Stevenson, the family that has dominated fishing in Newlyn for several generations and owners of one of the largest privately owned trawler fleets in the world.

"The mackerel went of their own accord," David is certain, and is sure that fishing effort was not enough to have any great effect on the stocks. "There was just too much there to be able to exterminate them all. Their migration patterns change from year to year, and they just left and took themselves elsewhere."

While David Stevens was one of the Stevenson family's top skippers, he saw the end of the pelagic fishery for Cornish boats with two winters' midwater trawling, spent two summers scallop fishing, and took part in the opening up of the south west fishing grounds for beam trawling.

"Frankie Knowles was beaming, and David Hooper was skipper of the *Algrie* and I was mate with him. Then Billy Stevenson bought the *AA* (*Aaltje Adriaantje*), and I took the *Algrie*, which was the first of the Dutchmen that he bought."

"It was a new fishery and new fishing grounds. We started fishing south of the Scillies, and we used to get monks like you've never seen,

139

megrims like cricket bats, and a sprinkling of roundfish. There was a lot of fish on that ground at the time," David said with something of a faraway look.

"I just got tired of beam trawling, it was too easy. Sometimes you'd go whole trips without having to take your slippers off. At least now I'm out on deck as well and getting a bit of fresh air."

David skippered Stevenson's beamers for six years, and was the Newlyn fleet's top skipper for several of those years, before going back to the family business in partnership with his brother Peter 'Skull' to skipper the *Rose of Sharon*, which was netting at the time.

"I hated netting, so we had a hopper trawl made up, a net with 14 inch hoppers and we opened up the grounds north of the Scillies, all virgin ground then. We used to catch plenty of fish, and it was good money compared to how things are now. The last year I was skipper of the *Rose of Sharon* we grossed £190,000. By 1989 we were in a position to get this boat, and my brother carried on with the *Rose of Sharon*."

The brothers fell out after a while, and the two boats now operate separately. David had some difficult years with the *Crystal Sea* to begin with, dogged by breakdowns and engine trouble before he was able to get on his feet properly.

"The first trip trawling was a £3500, landing in August 1983, plenty of fish and a lot of crayfish. We've had some good years," he said with a smile. But at present things are not so bright.

Leaning over the chart table in the *Crystal Sea*'s wheelhouse, he swept a hand over the western approaches to show roughly where the seasons take the boat.

"It's November now, south of Newlyn, and the occasional trip to the 'Ships once in a while," he said, indicating the Longships lighthouse. This is the hard ground just west of Land's End, where the heavy trawl gear on the net drum comes into its own.

"We're further off by February, March time, and follow the spring fishing south of the [Scilly] Islands. By June we'll be north of the Islands on the hard ground where the beam trawlers work. I'm not saying we don't go other places as well, sometimes you'll get a week of big tides and have to go back to the clean ground, but that's roughly where we'll be fishing over the year."

By that afternoon, with the *Crystal Sea* not far off the land, the wind had freshened even further, and the full rig of oilskins were called for on deck. The lush green of the Cornish coastline around Mount's Bay was dappled with patches of shadow from the driven clouds that dotted the otherwise bright blue sky, and the biting wind was far from being in keeping with the bright sunshine. White horses had appeared over the day, and the cold November breeze stung cheeks and fingers, and brought some icy spray over the stern as the doors were unclipped.

"There's no need for that," Tuc complained as a burst of spray through the shelterdeck hatch caught him full in the face as he stood there with the gilson in his hand waiting for the codend.

"Not more than a basket of fish there," David announced as the codend was emptied onto the deck. "We'll get the gear aboard."

Leaving the fish where they were for the moment, Tuc went aft and Boy David collected an extra waterproof top before making his way aft. David at the controls swung the powerblock into place, and the ropes around the body of the trawl were wrapped around the drum, hauled on until they had a purchase, and the wings were swung in one at a time, with Boy David and Tuc hauling handfuls of netting to bring everything inboard.

"There's some debris there," Boy David called, as the footrope came fully clear of the water. Hauling slowly, David brought the gear out of the water and brought to light a jagged piece of steel, several feet across, that had been caught up in the footrope. Struggling with the size of the chunk of metal, and with efforts to keep a steady footing on the moving deck, they bundled it aboard, stowing it clear of the trawl to be disposed of ashore.

The light footrope with its small rubber discs was stowed away in the pound and the bulk of the netting dropped on top in bights, Tuc and Boy David hand over handing netting as fast as they could, and the belly and codend coiled on top. The doors followed, lifted inboard using the powerblock and dropped inside the gunwales, where they were lashed tight to the gallows.

With the gear secure, Tuc and Boy David went forward to gut the few fish in the haul, and to ice them down, while David in the wheelhouse set a course for Newlyn, an hour's steaming away. Watching the *Crystal Sea*'s progress, he called the boat's agent on the cellphone to give a tally of the fish on board, ready for the next day's market, ordered ice and fuel for the next morning, arranged to hand over the trip's pot bait to a crabber, and called one of the other boats to let him know that it was time to call it a day.

"We have an arrangement between ourselves. If I need towing in, he does it, and if Merv needs to be towed in, I do it. But he'd better not need me in the next day or two, because we won't be here."

Crystal Sea punched for an hour and a half through the freshening sea and steamed into the calm of Newlyn harbour in the late afternoon, with the sun already setting and evening coming on. David brought the boat slowly along the length of the harbour and past the lines of beamers and crabbers still moored up, bringing her in to tie up next to the ice plant where the trip had started.

The ice plant's manager stood on the quay and spread his arms in protest as Boy David and Tuc put the ropes ashore to tie up.

"I've told you that I was going to put the boat here," David called out of the wheelhouse window. When I ordered the ice you told me that you'd finished icing the netters and there'd be no more today."

"But what if somebody comes along and wants ice?"

"Like I told you before, I'll be aboard the boat and we can move if needs be."

Another protest followed from the quayside, and David pushed up the heavy sheet of toughened glass in the window shut with a finality that ruled out any further protests. The fatigue of a week at sea with never more than a few hours' sleep at a time was showing in David's face, and he was clearly not going to be argued with.

"That's just what you need after a week at sea, some idiot telling you what to do like that."

David, Tuc and Boy David set to on the fishing gear, mending tears in the trawl's belly and overhauling the codend for the next trip. David worked fast, cutting out and braiding into holes in the net with a deceptive speed.

"That's all right there now. Can we have her up a bit, please Tuc?"

Not used to the powerblock's controls, Tuc took several attempts to manoeuvre the hydraulic arm to haul up another length of belly, guided by shouted instructions from David, until another section of the net was in position to be overhauled. Then the process began again, folding back armfuls of net to identify holes or patches where the net was too worn to trust, cutting out and braiding new net into them, stopping now and again to fill more needles, working from the codend forward to the tips of the trawl's wings.

Despite being ashore late in the afternoon, none of the crew expected to be at home until the following day. "We'll stop on the boat tonight and land in the morning, then we can take our ice and be home after that. Sail on Sunday and hopefully the weather should be all right for a couple of days in the week."

With the trawl overhauled ready for the next trip, David and his crew made their way back inside for the evening meal, a huge stew prepared by Boy David on the way back to Newlyn, with solid chunks of meat steaming in a mass of vegetables and helped down with bread doorsteps.

As I packed my oilskins away for the journey home, the *Crystal Sea*'s crew were taking it easy for a couple of hours before turning in, expecting to be up at five the next morning to land their fish for the next

Crystal Sea tied up by the ice plant in Newlyn at the end of the trip.

day's market. Choosing a landing day can be a tricky business, and David and Robin the agent work closely together to put fish onto the market on the most promising days. In general weekday markets are preferred, and there are many factors that can go into a catch fetching a good price, not least the number of boats landing on the same day.

"We once had a big fleet of netters in Newlyn, and if they all came in to land together the prices would drop, so you had to be careful to land between their landings" David explained. "If you had 50 netters landing over two or three days, it's some volume of fish."

Hake netting has suffered a decline as stocks became scarce, and the same has happened with wreck netting, shooting nets directly over a wreck to catch the roundfish that accumulate around any obstruction on the seabed. The numbers of netters have fallen over the past few years, as boats have been decommissioned or sold away, leaving a nucleus of top catchers who have survived.

"Sometimes if you had a poor trip, you'd be tempted to clip a wreck at the end of it, and hope to get a good bag of fish," David explained. This can be a risk, and before the accuracy of Differential GPS, this could easily mean a day's mending instead of a bag of fish to finish a trip. "But now if you clip a wreck, there's nothing there. They've stripped it all out."

"I've seen the rise and the end of the wreck netting and the hake netting. I've seen different fisheries come and go, but trawling always stays. You get good years and bad years, but we still push through."

Many of the species that the south west trawlers target are now governed by quotas. Fishing for sole, plaice, hake, megrim, cod, haddock and whiting is all heavily regulated, but so far there are still non pressure stock species, and these make all the difference.

"About half of what we catch is non pressure stock fish, cuttlefish, squid, red mullet, skate, monkfish, turbot, brill and the like. If there were no quota fish left, we could just about muddle through on non pressure stock fish, if we had to," David said, leaving it unsaid that life would still be an uphill struggle to survive. Track records are vital, in case these species are subject to quotas in the future. Everything is carefully logged, including the non pressure stock species, against the day when Brussels decides that everything has to be a pressure stock species.

"I book 'em all out. We could make a living on non pressure stock fish, so things aren't so tight for us as they are for the beam trawlers. It has been a bad year, and it hurts, especially if you've got borrowings," David admitted." We're missing the cod, whiting and haddock. They haven't turned up this year. But it'll be back. I've no doubt it'll come back."